1

HOW TO BE 23

What No One Tells You About Adulting

HOW TO BE

23

What No One Tells You About Adulting

By: Lauren Allen

Dedication

Dear Samantha,

If I could take all of the pain in the world in order for you to never have to get hurt, I would. Instead, I dedicate this book to you in hopes that I can ease your journey by sharing my mistakes and how I got through them (some more easily than others). We may have spent most of our childhood butting heads over our vast differences, but in the end our arguments always pushed us to be more passionate about what we were striving for.

I want you to always be stubborn about the things you love, kind about the things you cannot change, and open to things you have not yet experienced. This world is so big, and you deserve to experience everything it has to offer.

So many times at 23 I called you to be my support when I needed you, and you were always there for me. For that I cannot thank you enough. I will never be done needing you, and I want nothing more than for you to lean on me when you need a little extra strength.

Your world will change so much before you hit 23, but every lesson learned along the way will be a stepping stone to the person God made you to be. Make every moment count, because every day is a blessing, which is reason enough to live life like there is no tomorrow.

"With God all things are possible." Matthew 19:26

Love,

Your big sister

Table of Contents

Prologue

Jet-lagged and exhausted, I rolled over with a sigh and plucked my phone from under my pillow while the bright morning sun peeked through the windows of my old and cramped Harlem apartment. It was 8 a.m., and my phone had more notifications than my sleepy eyes could focus on. These weren't the texts I expected to wake up to this day. The words were hurtful, threatening, coercive, and lies that were supposedly being spread about me from someone who just days earlier I had considered my best friend. Fear struck me like a bolt of lightning, and I instinctively held my breath as my hands began to shake. Would I be trapped in this painful universe forever? Was this my new reality?

Tears began streaming from my already red and puffy eyes. It took all of my remaining strength to pull the covers over my head and send myself back to sleep. I just wanted to forget the day and all of the events that had led up to it.

This was my birthday, May 24th, the start to my learning to be 23.

In the last 24 hours my life had flipped upside down like a burnt pancake. Just a day before I had been in California with a thrilling job, a boss who had become my best friend, and all of my career dreams coming true right in front of my eyes. In a matter of a few hours I went from having everything to having nothing but a seat on the next flight from LAX to JFK.

The next month became a spiral of hitting the bottom over and over. Just when I thought there was nowhere lower to go, I'd somehow find another ledge to fall off. It was also the month in which everything I thought was secure in my career slipped out of my hands and caught fire while floating through the air.

For months prior to this I had spent all day, every day pouring all of myself into this job, distancing myself from my friends, missing holidays with my family, and sleeping only a few hours every night.

The job brought me to Los Angeles, where I had once only dreamed of living. It opened doors to events and meetings I thought I would never see in person. Opportunity can be a double-edged sword. The presentation of these once-in-a-lifetime opportunities can be awe-inspiring, but in reality the picture-perfect moment is only made possible by sleepless nights, bad politics, and just a touch of manipulation. Sure, I could tell cool stories around the dinner table for years to come, but is it all worth it for the cost of my mental and physical health? That's a question that still lingers over me every day.

In the midst of my downward spiral I also had moments of forgetting my reason to live. Every penny I had saved to follow my dreams was drained, the career I had envisioned for myself seemed far out of reach, and I was just too tired to even stretch out my hand to ask for help.

Luckily, God already had a friend in place for me who stretched out her hand without hesitation. I hadn't seen my roommate, Dari, in months, and my unexpected trip back to our Harlem apartment was convincing enough for her to cancel all of her plans for the day. She dragged me out of bed and gave me time to be the hot mess that I was, but after that forced me to pull myself together, get dressed, and get out of the house.

With both of us being broke, we did what we could to make the day special. And by "we" I really mean Dari, whose patience shone through while toting me around town like a wet dish rag. We checked out the Met's fashion exhibit for which you choose how much you pay for admission (ten cents seemed reasonable to us), sauntered around Central Park in the early summer sunshine, and then splurged on five-dollar happy hour martinis.

As much as I fought the idea of forcing myself into a cute outfit, there's something about getting dressed that will always make me feel better in any situation. My outfit that day was courtesy of Dari laying my clothes out for me and handing me a tube of lipstick on the way out. Without her there would be no Instagram post to document this birthday.

This picture is the perfect example of how social media isn't always the reality of the person posting. But the real truth is shown in the art I chose to pose with. Of all the beautiful fashion at that museum, I chose to be photographed with the mannequins wrapped in what looked like wet dish rags. The designer perfectly emulated the vibes of my day.

laurenallenstyle
The Metropolitan Museum of Art, New York

That day I laughed, cried, reflected, and distracted myself. My 23rd birthday was the day on which my life changed forever, and I have Dari especially to thank for facilitating the changes that led me in the right direction.

It was after that day, in my reconstruction phase, that I learned to lean on my parents, my sister, and Dari as the rocks that they are. Some days they held me up as I had nothing left inside of me to prop myself on my own feet, and later on I found new bricks to build up the next part of my life.

Throughout the 18 years I had spent in school, I had always looked forward to being 23, because to me it meant being an adult, making my own decisions, and thriving in the career I had been working towards. In reality, I needed a support system more than ever as I grew into my newfound adult life.

For you this support system could be family, friends, roommates, or even a therapist if that is what it takes. There is nothing wrong with reaching out for help when you start to feel overwhelmed.

During this time you should be taking risks and reaching outside of your comfort zone, which means that you will probably fall on your ass (hopefully not as hard as I did), and you are going to need a team with you along the way to pick you up and dust you off.

Don't be afraid to stretch out your arm for help from that support system, even if it is six times daily during the bad days. I can assure you that they would rather hear from you all day than never be able to hear your voice again.

Just one year after this mess, I am now happier than ever before, working a job I love and thriving in the city of my dreams. This does not mean that I am done making mistakes, but I am now better equipped to learn from those blunders. Some days are better than others, but I know who to call when I need a shoulder to cry on or pom-poms to cheer along with me.

INTRODUCTION

As millennials we have been taught that the point of working hard for good grades in high school is to get into the colleges of our dreams. After college you're supposed to get a job in the area you studied. But then what? You live happily ever after?

Throughout school we all dream of the next step after graduation. Envisioning the rest of our lives after college can be so exciting, as anything can happen. We learn about all of the different career choices available to us and that if there's a gap anywhere in a field you are interested in there is always the choice to create a totally new position.

If you have been surrounded by positive people you have heard that you can do anything you put your mind to. The world is open to you, which should be the most thrilling possibility, but is that not also the scariest idea someone can give you? Schooling teaches us what is possible with what the world consists of right now, but what if the path you are meant for doesn't exist yet?

In order for millennials (born 1980 to 1994) and Generation Z (born 1995 to 2013) to have any hope of success we have to be good at a little bit of everything. The catch is that there is no way to study everything in college that we will need to know post-graduation. A big part of college is learning *how* to learn so we can take that and later apply it to our career path of choice. This is also when you will find your strengths and weaknesses.

One of the first required college classes I ever took was called "College Success," where we basically just learned how to take multiple choice tests on Scantrons, find the free pizza around campus, and use the school website to map out our schedules for the rest of our college careers. (This is a massive generalization of the class, but you get the idea).

My biggest takeaway from that class was hearing my professor regularly say that we needed to study abroad before graduation. I remember thinking that was not for me because all I wanted was to graduate as quickly as possible so I could free myself from small-town life and move to New York City.

Just a few months later my dad was offered a new position within his company that moved our family from Gainesville, Florida to Lexington, Kentucky. One small town to another. Even though I was already in college and over 18, I followed along because at the time my biggest fear in life was getting stuck in Gainesville. This seemed like a crazy decision to some people, but it was the right decision for me.

A few years and completely different states later I was sitting in a lecture hall at the University of Kentucky in my graphic design class. A guest lecturer stood up and told us about a study abroad opportunity in Italy that would complete the digital art minor I was working towards. I was instantly brought back to my College Success class and knew that for some reason this was the trip that God had been planning for me all of those years, despite my initial resistance.

On the bus ride home that night I created a presentation for my parents about how this trip would help me graduate sooner, practice living alone before my official move, and give me a once-in-a-lifetime opportunity. It took some convincing for my mom, but my dad was immediately on board. Just a few months later I was on a flight to Florence with 49 strangers to spend a month taking pictures and traveling the country. This trip was my favorite part of my college experience and the first time I really felt like I heard God's voice pushing me to do something I would have never done before.

A College Success course can tell you how to survive college and push you to try something you may have never tried on your own, but no professor can tell you what major is best for you when you are not yet quite sure what your path will look like. The important factor is that you can change your mind!

My first declared major was psychology because I liked to talk to people about their problems. It seemed like a practical option in which I could own my own business and look great while doing so. This lasted until I failed my second phycology class and realized that, as many classes as I could take to teach me how to use a Scantron, I will never be a skilled test taker.

From there I made a hairpin turn into the journalism department and found my way along that path. At that time I was falling for the fashion industry, but without a clear view of where that would take me my parents encouraged me to pursue something more broad to help me navigate the twists and turns of the future. My parents were happy that I was earning a "respectable" degree, and I was happy because I never saw a Scantron again.

General degrees like business, English, or fine arts are typically more open to interpretation. Even my journalism program offered widespread career choices upon graduation. Some of my peers were going on to law school, some wanted to teach history, and some aimed to become sports broadcasters. Then there was me, who proudly stated over and over again that I would be a fashion stylist in New York City as soon as I got my hands on my degree. There was nothing anyone could ever say to me that would make me want to work for the New York Times as a political journalist.

To me the more clear-cut degrees, like nursing, engineering, and computer science, hold to the more traditional mindset that you study this, then you get a job here, and then you grow within that field. This is not to say that focused degrees are not just as scary to follow through with, but they are just not a topic I feel like I can touch on because to me those were never an option.

A majority of my initial college education was more algebra than How to Do Taxes 101, linguistics rather than résumé building, and history instead of Decision Making for Dummies. Let's just say that taxes are a foreign language to me now and linguistics class was my way of avoiding four semesters of Spanish.

Once I got past the general education classes the lessons got more specific, and my interest levels peaked. These upper-level courses felt more practical for my future career, regardless of which direction I would take. There were still classes I complained about, but the overall experience felt right for me.

College taught me many lessons on decision making, time management, and how to find new opportunities. Graduating and moving to a big city to start my career taught me that I will never be done learning.

I have fallen flat on my ass (both metaphorically and physically) more times than I wish to count since leaving my Kentucky bubble, but it's the first step I take after picking myself up that starts my stride into my next greatest adventure.

In this book I will be sharing some of the lessons I had to learn the hard way by showing you my best attempt at making lemonade out of the lemons that hit me over the head when I thought I was under an apple tree.

Life isn't always going to be "happily ever after," but in each situation you have the choice to learn and grow. That's not always going to be easy, and sometimes a bad day is just a bad day. The first year after graduation is the perfect time to try new things, make mistakes, and maybe even find an entirely new career, like I did.

23 was possibly the most dramatically life-changing year I have yet experienced. It's possible that I will look back in 20 years and think, "Damn, that was nothing!" but right now it doesn't feel like nothing, and I think most of you feel the same way, which is why this book exists.

Growing up I was not much of a reader, but now that I am out of school I turn to books as a way to either escape the stress of the world or to learn how to deal with it better. The problem I came across was that there isn't enough published work available from authors my age. Everything I read comes from people who are much older and more established in their careers writing about their younger years and how they got to where they are now.

In an attempt to "speak it into the universe," as people say, I started repeating almost daily that I would write a book one day. For probably a year this just meant that once I did something that made me significant somewhere I would write a book about my journey. Maybe at 30 I would be experienced enough to write a book. Then I got to thinking, just the first year after college is enough to throw someone into a tizzy searching for answers. That brought up the question, why wait until I'm 30 when I have something to say right now?

If you are reading this it's probably because you are about to graduate and want to know what to expect, you just graduated and are freaking out about what to do next, or you remember how stressful 23 was and want to see how our lives compare. If you don't fit into any of those categories I hope my ridiculous stories are just some good entertainment.

23 was the most constructive year of my life, and for almost every person I've ever discussed it with it was a year of new perspectives for them as well. I often found myself angry that no one had prepared me for what was to come or that I should have been told the right things to do and say in order to avoid making mistakes in the first place. Although there is no real way of avoiding these growing pains, my goal is to share some of the lessons with you that I learned at 23. I swallowed a whole

lot of haterade, but now I can share the tips that I wish someone had told me before I dove head-first into adulting.

Chapter 1: Popping Bubbles

L ife after college is all about popping comfort bubbles (along with the occasional champagne bottle) and stretching yourself further than you could ever dream of. Some of it is going to take you to your breaking point, and some will give you wings. Sometimes it's even at that pivotal breaking point that your wings are freed.

What is absolutely true is that you will be forever evolving, becoming a new you every step of the way. Your job is to embrace the challenge and do everything you can to land on your feet as a better person than you were when you took the leap out of your comfort zone.

Sometimes the air will be choppy, the fog will cut your visibility, and the rain will slow you down, but all of those bumps will make you stronger for the next obstacle you come across in your journey.

It's hard to believe, but in the end you will look back and be thankful for all of the complications you came across because they each taught you something new that you would have never needed to learn if it was smooth sailing the whole way. Without the bumps you would never be thrown outside of your comfort zone.

My bubble exploded the day I packed up my life into a rented SUV and drove with my dad from Lexington to New York City.

Life in Kentucky was pretty good. I went to school without any loans thanks to my family, lived at home to save money (and to avoid learning how to cook), and had a few different jobs around town to keep me busy.

It was a big-fish-in-a-small-pond scenario. In my small(ish) college town I was on the board of directors for the Lexington Fashion Collaborative, produced fashion shows for the largest bridal show in the city, ran (and still run) a fashion blog, and was even the key stylist for the University of Kentucky's fashion magazine, KRNL Fashion. From a résumé standpoint, I was kind of a big deal in Lexington. I really had everything I could ever want in a career for a young adult dreaming of working in fashion. Except it all felt like nothing while jumping into a bigger pond.

It appeared to me that there are generally two kinds of dreamers in this world: the people who just daydream about what they want, and the dreamers who wake up and turn their dreams into reality.

When I would tell people I was moving to New York after graduation they would say, "That's nice" or "Bless your heart" with disbelief in their eyes. This was the added fuel to my fire of determination that pushed me towards my goals.

In college I spent a lot of time hearing other people's dreams of working towards their career goals, but I was continually disappointed when I couldn't see their progress. To me they were the reason no one believed me when I said I was moving to New York. Although no one else's opinion really matters, we all know that negative thoughts can rub you raw.

Any time someone told me they wanted to work in fashion it became my main goal to give them every opportunity possible to grow in that career. I was spending more time focused on the fashion opportunities in

Lexington than whatever it was I was learning in my classes at the time, and I wanted everyone to feel that same excitement I did.

"Come to a Lexington Fashion Collaborative meeting with me!"

"Get involved with our school fashion magazine!"

"Start a blog about your favorite campus trends!"

After a while I would get discouraged because no one was joining me in the adventures that brought me so much joy. If I loved all of these things wouldn't everyone else? It took me some time, but I finally realized that, although these things were my dream, they weren't everyone's dream. There are so many things to do in the fashion industry, and not all of them involve writing or styling.

Styling gave me so much joy in Lexington that, in my head, nothing could ever top it. By my one-year mark in NYC, after working as an intern, assistant, and then key stylist, I stepped back to see what I had done and the direction I was heading. It was then that I realized a celebrity styling career wasn't for me. This was also a moment of realization regarding how a career in fashion can look different than I had always envisioned it. Making a full career change is one of the scariest possible moves after spending years thinking you knew exactly what the rest of your life would look like.

My hope is that maybe you won't have as many growing pains as I had along the way, and if you do you will know that you are not alone and that God has a great plan for your life.

In order to get stronger you must create tiny rips in your muscles to make room for more muscle to grow. The pain of lifting weights and being sore the next day sucks, but we do it for the reward of being stronger in the future. Moving to New York City was like taking on a bodybuilder's workout regimen after referring to carrying shopping bags as exercise for three years. It took a lot of self-motivation, weight dropping, and tears to get where I am today. And trust me, I still have a long way to go.

Chapter 2: Pre-23

My side-hustle life started at a young age when my mom was a Mary Kay sales director. She would hold open houses during the holidays for customers to come and buy gifts for friends, family, and themselves. When I was little I'd stand in the guest bathroom and show people how to use Satin Hands, which is a four-step exfoliation and moisturization process. It not only smelled amazing, but it was also heavenly feeling.

I would make commission (from my mom) off every Satin Hands set I sold for her. This brought out the selling monster in me that constantly wanted more. If I could sell in our guest bathroom, why couldn't I sell to a table full of women in our dining room? By my early teen years I was begging my mom to let me teach the skin-care classes. She started me out slow with mother/daughter events in which the group would separate and I'd get to work with the daughters. Soon I was taking over part of each class and on a total power high. There was nothing else I could ever imagine doing for the rest of my life.

Every week I'd beg to go to the meetings and watch the consultants get crowns, sashes, and awards for their accomplishments. At that point Mary Kay Cosmetics was the only business I knew, but over and over again I'd hear about the idea of a J.O.B. where the women would complain about their day jobs and work towards being able to sell Mary Kay full-time. The obvious answer to me was to avoid the real world and join the pink bubble as quickly as possible!

Until I was about 17 my only life goals had been to sign a Mary Kay agreement on my 18th birthday, win a pink Cadillac by 21, and become a National Sales Director by 25. This would mean I'd never have to answer to another boss, and I could wear pumps every single day.

This pink bubble was where I was rooted, and now that I have grown outside of the bubble, part of me is still drawn to the idea of not having a "J.O.B." and spending my life working for myself. This is not the life for everyone, but it is ideal for any creative person who wants to go down an unmarked path.

During my senior year of high school my mom joined a large networking group in Gainesville called BNI. At this point it was normal for me to go to work with her on a regular basis, which meant that I wanted to be a part of this network also.

Bright and early one Tuesday morning I put on my favorite "work" dress and followed my mom to the weekly networking meeting. Once I walked in I was taken aback by the huge room filled with 75 business owners and many long tables all facing each other in a large circle. At the time, I was easily half the age of the youngest person in the room, but that was nothing new to me after attending Mary Kay meetings my whole life.

For that first meeting I just sat back and took it all in. It can easily be intimidating to sit among a roomful of business owners and feel like you have nothing to offer them. I had also not been around men of power much during my life. Ten years of synchronized swimming and over 15 years of the Mary Kay pink bubble meant that the only man I had spent time with was my dad.

Once that first BNI meeting ended I ran to my first class of the day. I walked in feeling a sense of accomplishment in the fact that I had spent the morning in a room of adults who instinctively respected me because of of the confidence I exuded.

Looking around at the teenagers wearing sweatpants and numb looks made me realize that I had always wanted to surround myself with successful, hard-working people. To me this is what would exemplify how to be passionate about my career and never settle for anything less than the best.

There were times when the midterm paper took priority over a shower (college deadlines can be a killer), but I always saw it as a form of respect to the professors to show up to class looking like I cared about being in that room.

To the guy in his pajama pants at 3 p.m., though, I need to hear your excuse...

A few weeks after my first BNI experience my mom had to miss the meeting, so she sent me in as her substitute. This would be the first time I would have to stand on my own two feet and not use her as a shield to hide behind while taking in the meeting as an outsider.

Attending as a substitute meant I would have to stand up in front of the group, introduce myself, and speak for 30 seconds about the business I was representing. Although I was pretty sure I was going to have a seizure from shaking so much (if that's even a thing), I did it and came up with my next career bucket list item. I was going to become a public speaker. This is still a goal I am working on pursuing.

I guess I did all right because from then on I subbed for different business owners every Tuesday morning until I moved to Kentucky. By this point my mom had started to convert out of the Mary Kay bubble and into the world of bridal makeup. She is now the proud owner of Image Insight Makeup Artistry and Aesthetics (after going back to school for aesthetics). #PROUDDAUGHTER

I will forever respect and appreciate the experience I grew up with in Mary Kay because without it I would not be the person I am today. It was my experience at BNI that opened my eyes to the world of entrepreneurship in that owning a business means doing whatever makes you happy, not just following a business model that's handed to you in a welcome package.

By this point I had graduated from the entrepreneurship academy within my high school, was watching Image Insight bloom, and beginning my adventures of daily blogging.

My dad, being the computer nerd he is, had bought the domain laurenallen.com for me when I was a baby. Over the years I had played around with it, showing off a few of my random business ventures, like my jewelry-making business with my best friend Maria in middle school and a gift-basket-making business in high school, but nothing really stuck. Eventually I decided to start blogging; I wanted to test my writing skills.

Getting started was overwhelming and time-consuming. I didn't know when to write, what to write about, or who would care. After the one or two posts I had already written had not gone viral all on their own I tried to reason my way out of blogging. Before I could my dad confronted me with a personal test the competitive side of me couldn't turn down. He challenged me to write one blog a day every day for a week. We talked it through and decided the blog posts would revolve around my clothing choices, as this gave me a fresh topic daily and pushed me to put more effort into something I loved: putting together cute outfits.

In her book *The 5 Second Rule* Mel Robbins says, "Every stage of your life and career requires a different you." The idea of the five-second rule is that when you have to do something you don't want to you count backwards from five, and by the time you hit zero there is nothing left to do but move. A blast off! This action is what will drive you to the next, better you. Before I even read this book my dad, knowing what makes me tick, knew I needed a launching pad of my very own.

Starting in early May of 2012 my first blog photos were taken with the iPhone 4 in front of our kitchen pantry. It can be embarrassing to look back and see how bad the images were, how weird the outfits looked, and how awkward the writing was, but one thing is for sure: this one little challenge changed my entire life.

Outfit blog: Day 1

Seven days of consistent blogging quickly turned into 365 days of back-to-back posts. During this time I turned 18, went to prom, graduated high school, and moved to Kentucky. Some of my most important memories are documented on laurenallen.com for the rest of time, thanks to one night of brainstorming.

Although I never became "famous" from blogging, the lessons and memories are priceless. Writing *The Adventures of Lauren Allen* has been the starting block to launch me into the fashion industry and now writing this book. Without the almost 900 blog posts in the last six years there is no way I would feel prepared to write a book.

Blogging fueled my stride towards fashion and left me always wanting more. Constantly looking for new fashion opportunities, I came across a brand-new fashion magazine in Lexington called MOUR. After reaching out on Facebook the creators agreed to meet with me over coffee. During that meeting I learned that they were in the process of printing the first-ever edition of the magazine. After reading through my past work (on laurenallen.com) the ladies invited me to join their next creative meeting, where they would plan out the second edition of MOUR. At that point the only writing I had ever done was for my own blog and anything required in school. I was beside myself with excitement over being part of a real fashion magazine.

The nice aspect of this grassroots publication was that, despite how unqualified I was to write for a fashion magazine, they still wanted me involved. Maybe it was the desperation in my eyes that convinced them to give me a chance. Whatever it was gave me the push I needed to keep taking chances and get out of the blogging bubble I had created for myself.

My first writing assignment included a co-writer, which I could not have been more thankful for because that would have been overwhelming by myself. We wrote about vintage shopping in Lexington. This was not my strong suit at the time, but since then I've found a deep love for secondhand clothes! When it came time for the photoshoot that would surround our article we were asked to also pick the outfits from the vintage stores we had written about. On photoshoot day I was like a little kid on Christmas morning. I didn't fully know what to expect, but I knew I would be thrilled at whatever it was.

My co-writer and I had already put together all of the outfits; we just needed models and photographers. If I remember correctly I even ended up doing the makeup for the shoot that day! (Using my knowledge from assisting my mom in Image Insight for weddings and special events).

Being able to see the outfits we pulled come to life on set brought a tear to my eye. I was hooked. If I was that excited just watching the photos being taken, imagine my excitement when I found out that my favorite outfit would be on the cover of the magazine.

My first magazine cover!

The magazine grew exponentially, and before I graduated I had written articles for close to 15 issues. It was something out of a dream for a small-town fashion lover. I wasn't even 21 yet, but I was the lead writer for a fashion magazine! What MOUR really taught me was my love for styling.

The best part about it was that my school work and fashion work were colliding because of the classes I was taking. While all of my classmates were scurrying to get published somewhere at the end of the semester for class credit, I was handing over printed magazines with my name splattered throughout the glossy pages.

Did I have a social life? No. Did I have any friends my age? Not really. I was high on life, though, loving the fact that I was doing exactly what I wanted to be doing with my life before I even graduated. Just to be clear, though, I still let some classes slip between the cracks that I should have paid more attention to, and I was FAR from the perfect student. Luckily my teachers understood and respected my dream, worked with me, and pushed me to my fullest potential.

The peers I held closest in college came along during my senior year when I worked as the key stylist for our school's fashion magazine, KRNL Fashion. The day I got hired is one that will always bring tears to my eyes every time I think about it.

Looking back, this was overall one of the proudest and happiest times of my life. I knew this life wasn't sustainable for me, though; I was already feeling the glass ceiling of a small town. Life was great, but after college it was time to be a small fish in a big pond. MOUR Magazine took in a girl with no qualifications and no real knowledge of the industry and gave me the confidence I needed to know that I could do anything I put my mind to. It felt like a peak into the rest of my life.

Unfortunately, the magazine ran its course relatively quickly and dissolved after about two years. Although it's sad that MOUR is no longer sharing fashion with the bluegrass state, I will forever be thankful for what it shared with me.

In MOUR's absence I was searching for a new project to work on and quickly came across a business venture that allowed me to grow my styling business and try something new all at the same time.

Swept Away Proposals was a fun business adventure during my senior year of college that taught me so much about entrepreneurship. All of the businesses I had been a part of before had premade business plans ready for you to take and run with, but this took my business skills to a whole new level. It even allowed me to use what I learned in the entrepreneurship academy in high school.

I also learned a lot about working with business partners. There were four owners total, and I was honored to be one of them! The photographer, travel planner, makeup artist, and fashion stylist came together to create a business plan solely focusing on planning over-the-top wedding proposals. We got to the point of promo photoshoots and graphics (made in my graphic design independent study) and even a planned launch party that we never ended up having. The business plan was done, and we had everything we needed except the time to commit to a new business baby.

After graduating from the University of Kentucky the family I was babysitting for hired me as a full-time nanny. Their three kids were getting out of school for the summer, and with a fourth on the way they needed an extra set of hands. When the offer first came in it scared me a little because my fear was that I would see how much money was coming in and push back my move to New York. To counteract that I gave myself (and the family) a deadline. By the time the oldest kids went back to school I would be moving.

That summer I worked harder and more than I ever had before in the most unglamorous position I've ever held. I also was able to do some of the most exciting things I've ever done. We traveled, took boat trips, saw new things, and met new people. The kids taught me patience and love like I have never experienced before. Saying goodbye to them was almost as hard as saying goodbye to my own family when the summer came to an end. I had to leave to follow my dreams, but I absolutely left a little part of my heart back in Kentucky with them.

Chapter 3:
BOUNDARIES MAKE THE WORLD GO 'ROUND

Before moving to New York "boundaries" was just a scary word that couples in movies used to make sure their relationships weren't moving too quickly. The noun is put out into the world when men feel like the women they have been dating want to jump a level and pass go.

The boundaries I had to learn to draw the hard way have had more to do with work than dating. Too often I pushed the boundaries of "boss" and "best friend." Not being from a big city, I had a hard time differentiating between who to trust in a work environment. I have always trusted immediately and pulled back when I saw signs that made me question someone. This is probably because all of my work experience had been with my mom, through school, or with other people who had also never felt the need for these lines.

Sometimes it is already too late when the sign pops up. In retrospect I could have saved myself a lot of heartache if I had just started with a clear line between boss and friend.

- How to Be a Pushover -

I really thought that having a college degree and general common sense would be the perfect starting ground for my marathon of life in the big city. Since I'm writing this now, we all know I was terribly wrong.

When I moved to New York I knew no one other than some extended family that lived a few subway stops away from me. My roommates were from my hometown in Florida, but we never interacted outside of Facebook (you know, that social media where you go to get praise from all of your mom's friends about how beautiful and successful you are when Instagram just isn't cutting it). But that was okay because I had a plan.

After saving up all summer, I had enough money to live in the city (Harlem to be exact) for six months while working for free as a freelance intern fashion stylist. During this time I believed I would obviously become great friends with the other interns; we would all grow together and become assistant stylists at the six-month mark. From there I would be making great day rates, go out at night, and sleep in on the weekends. What a great life that would be, right?

It didn't take long for me to realize that this can be a very lonely city. I would show up to intern days and either be surrounded by assistants who thought they were above me or working alone while picking up and dropping off samples.

Not long after commencing my plan I met Charlotte.* She had just picked up a new celebrity client and needed some help. Of course, I was working for free for the experience, but as per usual I took on the job as if it were my own. It started out as a few hours during the day organizing clothes and picking up samples. Carrying full garment bags around the city and through the subway system was one of my strongest talents at this point.

(*I have changed all names and some details in this book so as to not harm anyone's reputation in any way. These experiences are my own and do not necessarily reflect the overall work ethics of the women I have worked for and with.)

So began some of the loneliest weeks of my life. I was the assistant stylist to a "celebrity stylist" and even getting to meet and go to parties with the client. From the outside I was living the dream, but in reality I was overwhelmed and alone.

I went from blindly fetching sealed garment bags to personally requesting pieces from every designer collection there is. There wasn't even time to pick up bags anymore, so I was begging the PR firms to messenger us the garments, and I would figure out how to return them after the event. Before long I even had my very own team of interns, some of them having been in the industry longer than I. In order to have everything together in time I had to rent out a storage unit. Yes, you did read that right. A concrete storage unit in the middle of Manhattan.

My "friends" at the time were the stylist I rarely laid eyes on, the messengers who brought me the couture I requested, and the salesman at the front desk of the storage unit who would let me sit in the lobby's corner to steal their wi-fi so I could send more emails. He was also the closest I got to a romantic date those days. Sometimes we ate our meals at the same time! If you consider a peanut butter and jelly sandwich a meal.

I worked from 11 a.m. to 3 a.m. every day, rarely taking time to eat, drink, or even pee. There was nothing glamorous about this life except the clothes hanging in the concrete storage unit.

And did I mention that this job wasn't paying my bills in the least? I stuck with this gig because I was sure that it was going to lead to a long, happy career, and I've never been afraid of hard work, so the hours didn't scare me away. It did, however, lead me to some very interesting experiences... but that's another story (or whole book in itself). This was the beginning of my lesson on boundaries. And no, this wasn't even the one that really hit home for me.

Considering we were working hand-in-hand, it wasn't long before I felt completely comfortable with Charlotte. She seemed like the ideal of what I wanted to be in just a few years, at least before I really got to know her. I had also never been hurt by a job before, so I only expected the best, since that's exactly what I was putting in.

Like many up-and-coming stylists, she required a side job at night to actually pay the bills. I would always work on my own assistant tasks while she was still around during the day, pick up where she left off at night, and then we would talk again when she got off of work to go over everything that still needed to get done before I officially shut down for the night.

My mistake here was becoming too friendly with my boss. No, not in any weird sexual way! More like I told her everything about my life— the good, bad, and ugly. I essentially gave her my whole existence on a platter and asked for nothing in return.

By the time photoshoot days or red-carpet days finally came around we had far surpassed all of our mental capacity and were essentially zombies. I was cranky and tired and never really got to appreciate the moment I had been looking forward to for weeks. There were even times I missed the experience altogether because it somehow became my responsibility to run some errands that took all day while an intern got the "on-set" experience.

The real problem I kept running into with Charlotte was her inability to decipher how much was appropriate to drink in different situations. This may sound crazy, as the general consensus is to not drink at work, but that rule is somehow blurred in the fashion/entertainment industry.

Having a margarita offered by a client at dinner is one thing. An entire bottle of port during a fitting is another. As much as I appreciate my lifelong nickname, Mamma Lauren, I don't so much appreciate taking care of the person who considers herself my boss when she's too tipsy to take care of herself.

Yes, fittings should be fun, but they are also still a time to focus and accomplish what you went there to do. Am I totally innocent here? Absolutely not. I also participated in the celebratory wine drinking (but cabernet though; port is nasty). What I didn't do, however, was surpass my limit. I always knew my boundaries when it came to alcohol and stayed within them, even at those stressful times when I wanted to just let loose. That had to wait until I was home with my roommate.

When I finally split ways with Charlotte she felt betrayed because I had allowed myself to be owned by her for too long. She was under the impression that I would be by her side for the long run, but in reality I was run down and had learned everything from her that I was ever going to learn.

She had no jobs lined up in the foreseeable future, and I had been given an opportunity that was irresistible at the time. Could I have broken the news to her in a better way? Maybe, but that doesn't mean it wasn't the right thing to do or the right time to do it.

Although I didn't realize it at the time, this was just the beginning of me questioning the industry. As an assistant the goal was to work up to being the key stylist. I realized later on that I in no way wanted to follow the path of Charlotte's life.

- How to Pick Up the Pieces -

The job that followed Charlotte is where I truly lost all boundaries, which means that I also lost the net that was waiting to catch me when I fell. From the outside my life looked like pure luck and fun. I went to some of the most spectacular events, wore stylish clothes, and even got to escape the painfully cold NYC winter for warm LA sun. A new city, a new position, and a new lifestyle that I had never seen before. This job was a quick side step away from styling and into personal assisting with the promise of styling jobs dangled in my face to hold my interest through the trudges of paperwork.

My first ever trip to Los Angeles was for the SAG Awards, but I spent most of my trip in a hotel room organizing the glam team. Just two weeks after that I was on another flight out of a blizzard and into the sunshine for the Grammy Awards and many music meetings. Less than a week later I was back again to help my new boss move a few blocks down the road. This trip was booked an hour before I had to leave for the airport and unexpectedly lasted almost four months. I spent most of that time either in yoga pants on the living room floor with my laptop in front of me and papers spread all around or dressed up in heels at a club you would hear about on reality television.

After attending one of the biggest music festivals in the country (one of the main items on my bucket list) I went home to Kentucky to visit my family for a few weeks. Although I was home, my work never stopped. I constantly felt torn between enjoying family time and the to-do lists that were being emailed to me from LA every day. My way of balancing it all was to accompany my family anywhere they went, but to have my computer with me at all times, working from the passenger seat. This was obviously not actual balance, but it was the only way I could keep myself from drowning. At this point I was a shell of myself, just trying to please everyone around me without taking care of any of my own needs.

The plan after my trip to Kentucky was to return to New York, but the song I had been working on publishing for this boss was finally launching, and I wanted to be around to see the the fruits of my endless labor. In reality there was very little celebrating and just much more work, but this did not really shock me at the time.
After the premiere I was promised an international trip, which is what kept me working in the height of some of the most stressful days of my life. Right before the trip the plans changed, and I ended up staying in LA while my boss went with a manager instead. I was upset, but I filled

the time by styling an actress for a few red carpets and events she had that weekend. Even though I was fully exhausted and hanging at the end of my rope, I felt like I was also living the dream I had painted for myself after graduating college and moving out of Kentucky.

I was a celebrity stylist (doing mostly personal assisting work) "jet-setting" between the coasts and attending all the coolest events with some of the biggest names in Hollywood. The reality of it, though, was that I worked for someone who would one minute tell me how much she loved and appreciated all of my hard work and then the next minute tell me how I was doing everything wrong and was the reason she was behind in her work. It felt like an emotionally abusive relationship that I did not see for myself until our fallout.

Any friends I had picked up since moving drifted away, I was making just enough money to pay my bills back in NYC, and I was barely sleeping. I dedicated 110 percent of myself to this job that I was nowhere near qualified for.

For a majority of my time in this position the aspect that kept me most motivated was the posse of people telling me I couldn't do it. My boss typically claimed to be on my side and helped me believe in myself—at least on the good days. Support like that created the false aura of trust and friendship.

There seemed to be something extra-motivating about having a group of "adults" tell me I couldn't achieve my goals because I didn't have enough industry experience. They saw me as a child, barely out of college, and unable to accomplish certain tasks solely because I had technically never done them before.

During this time I qualified myself to organize teams for red-carpet events, managing the debut of a new song and balancing the schedule of a musician. Multitasking became the usual, and creativity went out the door.

When my boss could tell that I was about to hit a breaking point she would give me a creative project to focus on, knowing administrative work is my weakest skill. Constantly working against my strengths was exhausting.

Because we were spending all of our time together we knew everything about one another, even things that no one else will ever know. We eventually became growingly annoyed with each other, even though we felt like we were best friends. Married couples would even have their issues if they spent as much time together as we did!

Being a woman who avoids conflict like the plague, I never brought up any issues I may have had and took punches as they came without trying to fight for myself along the way. Not being in my own city or really living my own life, I wouldn't dare do or say anything that would land me in a compromising position. This made our final fallout the most painful time of my life.

When she arrived back from that international trip I was left out of we were sitting on her couch catching up on the events of the weekend, and out of nowhere she accused me of something so painfully wrong I can't even repeat it.

Suddenly this one accusation spiraled out of control, and after pulling an all-nighter of arguments and groveling she assumed that everything I had ever told her was a lie. Words were said, items including prestigious awards were thrown (none by me), and my bags were packed. Hours later I was in the LAX airport when the texts started flooding in, asking where I was and why I wasn't begging for my job back.

I knew there was no going back from the damage that had already been done. My trust in her was broken, and she was pretty sure I was the most evil person on the planet. After all we had been through together I still had hope that maybe it would all end smoothly and we could wish each other luck with our futures, but that could not have been farther from the truth. The texts I received in the airport were just the tip of the sharp-edged iceberg. They went from asking me what she was supposed to do with all of the work I had supposedly left her with to threats of suing me for anything she could think of.

After being around her for so long I knew she knew how to throw direct daggers that could cut deep, but what I really didn't expect was for her to drag others into the war. On my birthday, after I stopped fighting, she followed through with her threats to reach out to my family and started sending direct messages to my mom through social media. The messages were fictional stories about things I had done, both work-wise and socially. My mom shielded me from that extra pain by not reading me the messages, instead just relaying what they said in generalized terms. Eventually she stopped opening the messages (or at least stopped notifying me about them) because every one only dug me into a deeper depression. I could barely take the messages coming directly to me, let alone the ones being sent to my mom in an attempt to tear me apart from my family.

Thank you, God, for the strong relationship my family has, which is unbreakable by outsiders trying to infiltrate.

After weeks of breakdowns, nausea, and panic attacks I was able to gain the strength to write a letter informing her that I felt like I was being harassed by her words and lies and that once this letter was sent she would be blocked on every platform I could think of. This ended the discussion, but my anxiety only got worse before it got better.

The abrupt end of that job left me unemployed (except for my wonderfully steady freelance work), without any savings, and just about friendless. I had been so invested in my job that I had no backup plan or even future goals.

I landed back at JFK in a million pieces, and all I wanted to do was crawl out of my skin and never look back. Luckily my roommate and my family stayed close, emotionally and physically when possible, to slowly glue me back together, even when I fought them every step of the way. Suddenly I went from no boundaries to a bulletproof wall.

This was my 23rd birthday and the start of my journey to true happiness, not just an Instagramable life. It wasn't easy, but the further I get from 23 the more the pain is just a memory and my smile is genuine.

- How to Learn When to Run -

After a few months of hiding I picked up an assistant stylist freelance job that was supposed to be a few days in an office, nothing hard, just some paperwork to wrap up a job that this stylist had just finished.

I was still in recovery mode but not ready to end my fashion career out of defeat. I wanted to make a clear choice that this wasn't the industry for me. I had worked with Kate in the past at my first paid assistant job. It was hell, and she knew it, which is why she specifically promised me that this time would be so much better. She had grown a lot as a stylist and even had a better office to work in this time around. I desperately wanted to turn down the job, but I needed the money more than ever before, so I agreed.

My first mistake was believing her promise of better conditions.

Kate told me the day rate, and I showed up to her office the next morning with no knowledge of what the next few days would entail. Her current assistant gave me a brief rundown of what needed to be done, and I got to work. Slowly I realized that this three-day job was going to take way longer than she had made it seem.

Her assistant had been so busy thinking about her upcoming move to LA, ready to get out and away from Kate forever, that she hadn't given me all of the information I needed. Every time I thought I was done I was given another dime of enlightenment that basically meant I needed to start all over again.

What I thought was going to be a quiet desk job to get me back on my feet dragged on for days and then even absorbed a separate styling job on top of all of the work I was drowning in already.

My second mistake was not running away with the first assistant!

After two weeks of working for Kate we were finally close to being finished. Kate, a different assistant, and I were all walking out of the office for the night when Kate asked if we were hungry. Being broke fashion assistants, it didn't take us long to agree to a free meal.

What we really wanted was a drink after this overwhelmingly stressful two weeks, so we ordered a round of martinis because what could that hurt? After polishing off our dinner and second round of drinks we left the restaurant, only to have Kate stop in her tracks one block down the street and declare her desire for another drink.

The right choice in this situation would have been to say, "Good night and good luck with that adventure," but remember, I was broke, overstressed, and naive, even after learning this lesson already.

We stopped into a chic hotel bar nearby, and before I knew it, it was 3 a.m. and Kate was drunk beyond reason. After the bouncers escorted us out in an attempt to close the bar Kate sat on the steps begging to be let back in. Eventually the bartenders called the cops to get her off the premise, and her response was to literally run from them as they tried to get her to go home.

Being the responsible adults in this situation, the other assistant and I stuck with her until we got her safely into a cab and on her way home. To accomplish this required us to run after her, sit on the steps of the bar waiting for her to come back, and search our emails for her home address to give the cab driver.

This was all after she had been speaking badly about me to the other assistant while belligerent at the bar, thinking I was out of earshot. She went on for an hour about how incompetent I was and how much better the other assistant performed her job than I did. If my confidence hadn't already been shot dead she may have woken up the next morning with a black eye.

Once Kate's cab was out of sight we went back to the office, collected any personal items we had left behind, and dropped our keys with the security guard. As we stepped outside to hail a cab home I dropped to my knees in a full-blown mental breakdown, sure that I would never work in the industry again but fully unsure about what to do with my life. By the time I got home the sun was rising, and I still had my weekly freelance work to finish by my morning deadline.

If this was my "comeback" after my 23rd birthday devastation I should just stop trying to do anything with my life, or so it felt at the time. This was not a situation I was mentally stable enough to handle, and it spun me straight back into a valley of depression.

All I could do was smirk later in the morning when Kate texted to say I didn't have to come into the office that day. As if there was any way in Hell I'd be there.

This was the night that truly taught me the value of separating work and play. If I had left work that night and met a group of friends out to get drunk this story would be much more reasonable. Instead it's disappointing and irritating.

Although I was right and did end up leaving freelance styling behind me, I did make sure to leave the career on a better note. After this job I picked up a few commercial jobs, which were light-hearted and all-around great experiences.

What I learned most from those jobs was that, even if I could do the work, it just wasn't where my heart was leading me. By the end of this job I had to trust that God had a plan for me that wasn't in the styling industry.

Chapter 4: Buses, Trains, Cars, and Motion Sickness

Despite all of my setbacks, New York City is still my favorite city in the entire world.

Sometimes I have to get out of town to regain the admiration I felt when I first moved here. After months of never-ending, smelly subway rides and tiny apartments with leaking ceilings it can be easy to forget what made me fall in love with this town in the first place.

When those moments wash over me I look for the nearest getaway option. Luckily for me, I have a lot of family in the New England area whom I have gotten to know better since moving to the east coast. My aunt in Florida called to tell me about a big family party that was to take place Mother's Day weekend in Connecticut. As fun as it sounded, my first response was that I couldn't take off of work, but I just couldn't stop thinking about the opportunity.

The hardest part about vacations for me, though, is biting the bullet and actually buying the travel tickets because then there's really no going back. I put off this step for a while until the Sunday after Cinco De

Mayo when my aunt called me with train times that worked with her schedule. On my last trip I had taken a bus because it was the cheapest option, but it was six long hours each way, and the fact that I get motion sick made the trip sound less appealing. This time around I had a little more money in my bank account and a determination to take the train like a working professional.

While booking the trip I was in a haze of the previous night's tequila and that afternoon's post-work nap (I had obviously compromised on my drinking-on-a-work-night rule for an important holiday!), so I just clicked on the links that looked good, typed in my credit card number, and got up to find a snack.

After work that Friday I ran to Penn Station and circled the building three times before tripping over myself in an almost-panic while running up the stairs to the Amtrak gates, just to read that the train was delayed an hour. I decided to make the best out of the situation by buying a new book and getting my freelance work done before my official vacation started.

The next day and a half were a blur of food, drinks, and family time. It's easy to feel alone living in such a large city, so from time to time it's nice to be fully surrounded by family, even if it's just for a few days. Before I knew it, it was time to head back to reality. A little hungover and a lot hungry, my aunt and and uncle drove me to the train station on their way to catch a flight back to Florida.

Severe motion sickness kicked in as I began the process of downloading my ticket in the backseat of their car, so I quickly tapped the last button and locked my phone to get back to looking at the horizon. We arrived at the train station just ten minutes before my scheduled departure time, which meant grabbing my belongings while quickly hugging my family goodbye and running inside.

Being unfamiliar with the train system, I approached the first person I saw who looked like he knew what he was doing and showed him my phone.

"Is this the train that's boarding now or in five minutes?" I asked.

He looked at me, furrowed his brows, and said, "Honey, that's a bus ticket."

Umm... What? I had definitely treated myself to a train ticket.

Dumbfounded, I asked him if he was sure, but he quickly rolled his eyes. He was officially over my dumb questions.

After looking at my phone to realize that it did, in fact, say, "Peter Pan Bus Lines" I felt that motion sickness kick back in, in full force.

Before allowing myself to fully panic I asked the annoyed man if this bus station was close, to which he agreed. So then, being an official New Yorker, I asked which way to walk to get there quickest.

"Walk?" He looked confused.

"Walk." My resolve was firm.

"No, you can't walk there!"

Oh. We're not in New York anymore, Toto.

I ran outside, finding it hard to breathe in the train station that I was obviously not welcome in anymore, and called my aunt in a state of horror and dismay.

"It's a bus ticket! I ordered a bus ticket instead of a train ticket!" I shrieked.

Being a typically calm and reasonable person, Aunt Paula had never heard me in distress before. This time around was a little different. She asked me if I was okay to find the bus on my own. My answer to her question was, "I don't know. I just don't know!" You'd think I was tied to the train track, not standing next to it a free and competent woman.

She informed me that, as much as she loved me, there was no way they could turn around and help me fix the situation or they would miss their flight back to Florida. For a moment I considered just saying, "Screw it" and going back inside to buy a train ticket, but there were much more fun things to spend my money on when I had already paid for transportation home.

With six-percent battery life on my phone and the slowest internet speed possible, I opened the Uber app, wondering what kind of service there would be in Providence, Rhode Island on Mother's Day.

The bus was leaving in three minutes, and I was three miles away. The clock seemed to be ticking faster than usual. I typed in an address I had recalled reading while opening the ticket earlier, and moments later a black BMW blasting rap music slid into the parking spot in front of me. This was my chariot to take me to the pumpkin of a bus ride home. I climbed in, nervously shoving my many bags and multiple coats into the backseat with me, and told the driver I had to be at the bus station before 3 p.m.

Through the rearview mirror I watched him furrow his brow and cock his head to the side as if I had suggested he provide me with a time machine, but the lack of blood in my face must have been convincing enough to attempt the impossible, and he revved the engine as I finished getting inside.

In my flusterment (if that's even a word) I slammed his door a little too hard, and we both went stiff.

"Ma'am, I'll get you there in time, but I'd like to have all four doors when you're done with me."

Awkward.

He accepted my apology, and we took off in a flash.

It was like the next Fast and Furious movie watching him swerve through traffic on that rainy afternoon. During our quick burst on the interstate I pulled up my ticket again to double check that I had the right address.

It was gone. I couldn't find any sort of address for where I was going within any of the documents I had in my email for this trip. It was too late to think about the possibility that we could be going to the wrong place, so I just trusted that God had somehow given me the right address at the right time.

He did, as I should have expected all along, and at 2:59.5 we pulled up to a Peter Pan bus. I'm not even quite sure that it's legal to pull up directly next to a bus at a bus station, but he did, and I ran up to the bus driver as he was closing the door, showing him the ticket on my phone, asking if I was in the right place.

A big smile grew across his face as he said, "Well, yes, ma'am, it is! It's your lucky day. We were just about to take off."

How lucky could I be if it meant I was about to spend my afternoon on a bus? But, regardless, in a ten-minute time period I had gone from running late for a train to being on time for a bus miles away.

Sparkly black-and-white-striped weekender bag, hot pink tote bag, and newly acquired vintage fur coat at my side, I climbed the steps onto the bus, realizing quickly that I was about to have to squeeze next to a stranger in order to have a seat.

So far out of it, I tried to drag everything horizontally through the aisle, knocking everyone on my left in the face with black sequins and everyone to my right with fur that had been in a closet for probably 40 years.

After looking through a good 20 rows I gave up on the idea of having a row to myself and plopped down in the first one that didn't have a bag in the way, piling everything I owned on my lap with a big "humph" escaping my lips.

So I did it. I was on the bus. Where was this bus going? How long was it going to take?

It also didn't take me long to realize how desperately I needed to pee and get out of this tight turtleneck and full-coverage bra. After the first stop, five minutes away, the bus driver announced that the next stop would be the NY Port Authority Bus Terminal in five hours. At that point I knew I was either going to get an infection or give in to the bus bathroom that the driver promised would smell like lilacs.

I didn't believe that for a second but was out of other options.

I pulled out my favorite Kentucky sweatshirt, shoved all of my belongings under the seat, and stumbled my way to the back of the bus, climbing on top of a sleeping man to get into the tiny bathroom that smelled more like a graveyard than a meadow of lilacs.

My first priority was taking off the bra that was suddenly tighter than a Victorian corset during social season and pulling on my cozy sweatshirt. Then I had to attempt to squat-pee because Lord knows what could have gone down in a Peter Pan bus bathroom before I got there. I was doing my best until the bus hit a bump in the road, throwing me backwards onto the toilet, and I gave up in another "humph" moment. A few squirts of hand sanitizer later I was back to my seat, defeated but homeward bound.

Before I knew it I was knocked out for a three-hour nap, probably becoming the person other people had to trip over to get to the bathroom. When I woke up I was thrilled to know that we must be nearing the city, which meant I was almost out of this motion sickness hell.

To my dismay we were stopped in traffic in the middle of a rain storm. It would be a few more hours before we saw another building. I plugged my phone into my computer to charge. The bus driver had promised free wi-fi, but that promise held just as much smoke as the promise of lilacs in the bathroom. Instead I closed my eyes and spent the remainder of the trip praying for it to go by quickly.

Excitement rolled over me as I saw us approaching my apartment building, not knowing that this was the direction we were taking! Unfortunately, even though we sat in traffic on my street for at least ten minutes, the bus driver could not legally let me off the bus early. Rules are meant to be broken, right? Apparently not for this guy.

With arms crossed and back slouched, the third "humph" of the day came out.

I was totally over it...

...Until we turned the corner at 42nd street and a perfect view of the New York City skyline appeared though the rain clouds. I was suddenly beaming. This is my home! This is where I am meant to be. All the frustrations of the day melted away with just this one picturesque scene.

I quickly hopped on the subway and made my way home, welcomed with a few Amazon Prime packages I had ordered before leaving town.

All was right with the world again.

Although I had been whiny for most of the day, as I tend to be when I don't feel well, the trip ended with me being eternally grateful for God's timing, my family, and the fact that I'm in a place in my life where I can take a weekend to travel on a whim.

What still hasn't changed, though, is that I do, in fact, have to make mistakes on my own, even dumb careless ones. But what I do know for sure is that I will never buy the wrong ticket ever again!

Chapter 5: Saying YES to a New Career

After my last major fall off the deep end (my 23rd birthday) I found myself on a job hunt. Cutting out a few industries, like restaurants and bars, anything that left me chained to a desk, and pretty much any freelance work, I decided to try out the bridal shops around town.

To be quite honest, I am not really sure how I landed on bridal shops as my point of interest. This was a dark point in my life, and most of my memory of the time is foggy at best. What I do remember is that it was the dead of summer and my hair was newly dyed purple. I put on my best "work" dress (a Banana Republic knee-length royal blue number with cap sleeves), tied up my hair, and hit the streets, résumés in hand.

A quick Google search had given me a laundry list of bridal shops in Manhattan, so I drew myself a map and worked my way downtown. At every store I stopped in I offered my assistance in any open position, preferably graphic design, web design, front desk, or consulting.

That weekend I was on a ferry to the local beach (bright green with motion sickness once again because ferries sound cool until you remember that you equally can't handle boats, cars, or buses) when an email popped up asking me to come in for an interview.

On Monday I re-pinned my hair in my best attempt to hide the purple, put on another business casual outfit, and hit the streets. This would be the last time navy cropped dress pants and a white button down would be work-appropriate in the bridal shop!

When I arrived at the store the manager wasn't expecting me, but she sat down for an interview with me anyway. She asked about me and my history, walked me around the store, and told me that every bridal consultant working there had over ten years of experience.

I had never sold a wedding dress in my life. Sure, I had zipped up a few brides while working for Image Insight, produced a couple of bridal fashion shows, and done a bridal photoshoot once, but I had never picked out a wedding dress for a bride-to-be.

At the time my self-confidence was pretty much down the drain, so I was sure there was no chance I was qualified for that job. I thanked the manager for her time and started to pack up my bag. Before I could stand up she looked at me and said, "Would you like to meet a few of your new co-workers?"

The day RK Bridal hired me my life changed forever.

- How to Look Past Pride -

While working at the bridal shop I have learned some lessons the hard way. Try to hold back your shock! Writing this book has made me realize how stubborn I am when it comes to making my own mistakes, as you can already see.

One day a bride came in while I was finishing up with another appointment. My manager pulled me to the side and gave me a warning look that only Jacqui can pull off. She told me that my next appointment was seemingly unpleasable, as she had been to countless other bridal shops, tried on hundreds of dresses, had an unlimited budget, and was never completely happy with anything she was presented with. It was obvious that the bride and her mother walked in with a heavy chip on each of their shoulders that they were perfectly happy to hold on to.

After a few weeks of being a bridal consultant and about a dozen dress sales under my belt my confidence was through the roof, and this was a challenge I was ready to face head-on.

The bride was a size two, so our size 12 samples were going to swallow her whole until I clipped the back to show her what the front would look like.

As I put her in the first gown I pulled from the sales floor her face lit up and she was sold. This lace fit-and-flare gown with thin straps was everything she was looking for. We talked colors and dates, but what I didn't bring up was the back of the gown that was curled up inside the hot pink spring clamps. She didn't seem concerned, so neither was I.

By the time she was filling out her order form she was on cloud nine. Her mom was hugging me, and I could see the weight of this decision being lifted off the bride's shoulders. I was gushing with pride at my ability to please the unpleasable. It all came crashing down when she saw a picture of the back of the dress. Apparently she could never walk down the aisle in a dress that was low enough to show her nonexistent tramp stamp.

Oops!

After going back to the drawing board and trying on other dresses nothing compared with the first favorite, and since the problem was unfixable according to her seamstress, whom she called in a panic, she left disappointed. It didn't help that my spirits were down as well. That was the first day at RK Bridal that I truly wanted to crawl into a corner and cry the day away.

This was my mistake to own, learn from, and never let happen again. Now I talk every bride through the back of every gown she puts on, whether she asks or not.

--- How to Take the Blame ---

It wasn't my fault...

Another day in the shop I had the sweetest client come in with just three dresses she wanted to try on. She brought her mom, her sister, and her credit card. This beauty was ready to find her gown! We tried on all three and came back to the second favorite.

Her mom was overjoyed that her little girl had chosen the wedding dress she had picked out for her. We spent some time finding the perfect cathedral veil with a lace trim to match the dress. Once all of the details had been attended to we started on the order form.

My manager wrote down the details with a questionable look on her face but didn't say anything to concern the client. As my sweet bride changed out of her gown with stars in her eyes and an ear-to-ear smile strewn across her face my manager pulled me aside to tell me the bad news. The dress was discontinued, and the only way she could have it was if she bought the sample, which was three sizes too big. The company hadn't sent us their latest discontinued list, which meant that we were in the dark until we went to place the order.

As I told the family I watched their glowing faces turn gray with disappointment. My heart dropped to the floor.

Luckily these women trusted me enough to start the appointment over, and we eventually found her a dress she loved even more than the first, but they never *really* looked me directly in the eyes again. The second appointment was significantly more somber than the first.

This mistake was out of my control; there were no indications on the tag for me to have known that this gown was no longer being made. The pattern had been destroyed forever.

Regardless of who was to blame, I still carried that weight on my shoulders for the rest of the day. Now the girls at the front desk always laugh when I check on every single dress before the bride says, "yes," to avoid that ever happening again.

Both of these situations really put a black cloud over my head, but that is only because I invest all of myself into every part of the job. If I sat back and said to myself that none of it matters because it's not my name on the door I wouldn't be heartbroken when a bride leaves empty-handed.

But I also wouldn't feel the joy that overtakes me when someone comes in and says they had a terrible experience at another store and the service I gave them was better than they could ever ask for. Yes, I do even cry with them when they say, "YES!"

There's also nothing like the joy of being invited to the weddings of the brides I get particularly close to over our time working together. Even if I don't actually attend the wedding, it's always nice to know they loved the experience with me so much that they want me to be an even bigger part of the most special day of their lives.

I mess up every day. Like, every single day. But rather than getting angry that I got caught or just angry at myself in general for making a mistake, I use those mistakes to be better the next day. Trust me, I'd like to just know the right thing to do all the time, but that's just not going to happen without a lesson learned.

After college you're going to make mistakes that impact more than your grade in a class. They will ripple through the company you work for, the customers you are serving, and the jobs of your coworkers. Most of the time these will be honest mistakes, and from everything I have learned the most important course of action is to be honest about the mistake.

Covering it up or trying to talk your way out of it never works. The quickest and easiest solution is to admit what you did and figure out the best next step to fix it. Most of the time this requires swallowing your pride, which could be hard to get down, but it's fully worth it in the end.

You are just starting your career; create a solid foundation for yourself. Constructing a house on the shore may look beautiful, but it's sure to wash away at the change of the tides.

Chapter 6: YOU ARE GOING TO BE UNDERQUALIFIED

Remember when you were told to go to college because that's the only way to get a job? Well, whoever told you that did not tell you the full truth. With more millennials earning bachelor's degrees than any previous generation your degree is just about as useful as a coat rack. Some may use it, but most just forget it in the corner, and it starts to collect dust. This may sound harsh, but I'm not saying you shouldn't get a degree. That is usually a necessary stepping stone. Completing a bachelor's degree wasn't even a choice in my household, and I am thankful that I was able to attend a great school. That degree is just not the only step along the path to getting a job. There are many more obstacles and complicated equations to configure before landing the job of your dreams.

What the big, bad, mean real world will tell you is that what you will need to get a job is experience—even for an entry-level job. You may ask, "How does one get experience without being able to get a job that requires experience?" That is an extremely relevant question that I and almost everyone my age have asked before. The real answer is that it is all about the way you phrase your experience and your confidence in the interview process.

You know your own abilities. Chances are high that you can do way more than the basics your skin-and-bones résumé shows. If your résumé listed every skill you have it would be too long for anyone to read.

Most of us are not qualified for any of the jobs we are striving to get right out of college. Every step along the way to your dream position will give you another skill to add to your portfolio of abilities. Even the smallest skill could make a huge difference for the job you are applying for.

The only way to get your foot into that first job is to win over the interviewer with what you have to offer them that the other person being interviewed right after you may not have.

You didn't just work the register; you provided excellent customer service for the clients as the last point of contact before leaving the store and deciding whether or not to bring their business back there. As long as you put your all into whatever job you have, it is easy to gain new skills every day that you will implement in your future career.

Also, before your interview, conduct research on the company you will be interviewing with. Know the position you are being hired for; know the right words to use and the right topics to cover when they say, "Tell me about yourself!" Keep the conversation focused on relevant topics that would persuade the interviewer to want to hire you.

One more thing: *always* bring a copy (or a few copies) of your résumé to the interview, even if you've already emailed it, faxed it, or dropped it off previously. Just always have it on you. Recently someone was interviewing for a manager position at the bridal shop. Before the manager started the interview she asked for a copy of his résumé to read over, but he didn't have one on him. In my eavesdropping my first (unsolicited) instinct was to cancel the interview all together. That may be a little harsh, but I think that if you can't bring a copy of your résumé with you to the interview it can make the interviewer concerned about your ability to manage a group of employees successfully. At least that was my concern.

I have gotten jobs before that I had no business getting just because I looked and sounded the part and showed confidence in my ability to do that job as well as the other employees who had ten plus years of experience. It's all about your posture, smile, and tone of voice.

Dress for the job you want in the future, not necessarily the job you're applying for. Are you interviewing for a front desk position but really want to run the company one day? Dress like you could one day be your interviewer's boss! The way you carry yourself speaks before you do in an interview setting.

Am I the only one who heard that a million times growing up? Maybe I had a strange childhood, but every time I think about applying for a job that is exactly what crosses my mind.

"You never get a second chance to make a first impression."

- How to Get Started -

Before my move I started looking for job opportunities to get me on my feet as soon as I landed in New York. To find those jobs I went through a stylist certification program called School of Style that puts its graduates on an email list for intern and assistant stylist job openings. Usually these were freelance jobs that lasted anywhere from one day to one month. The idea was that you get connected with the key stylist and continue to work with him or her for their other upcoming jobs, like photoshoots, red-carpet events, or commercial styling. This was how I found almost all of the styling jobs I ever worked.

One day a lead came in that excited me more than any other before it. This was also the first one I had ever responded to, considering I had not

64

yet moved to the big city. The stylist was looking for an assistant, but instead of for one shoot it was a more permanent position. Emails from School of Style landed in my inbox a few times a day, so there was nothing significant about the request except that this was not just any stylist. The sender was a past celebrity stylist and current fashion YouTuber I had admired for years. We'll call her Laura.

I knew Laura lived in LA, and I was about to move to NYC, but something inside of me said to apply for the position anyway. The email went something like this:

> Hello Laura,
> I received your email searching for an assistant. Although I know that you live in LA, I am preparing to move to NYC in the next few weeks and would like to offer my services to you in any way possible. From watching your YouTube channels and social media for years, I know that you go to New York Fashion Week every year. I apologize if that sounds creepy. If you are ever in New York and looking for help I would be honored to be that set of hands.
> Best,
> Lauren Allen

Then I attached my résumé and an additional cover letter (because you never send a résumé without an attached cover letter), said a quick prayer, and hit send.

Before I knew it I was on a Skype call with this stylist I idolized. She saw my fashion blog on my résumé, along with "web design" listed as one of my skills. At the time she was not happy with her website assistant and was looking to replace her.

This wasn't even the position she was originally looking to fill!

The job would consist of me posting her bi-weekly outfit blog posts and weekly YouTube videos on her website. This was something I had done hundreds of times before. Although I had not even moved out of

Kentucky and had never worked a day in New York, she took a chance on me.

For the first six months of our contract I worked as an unpaid intern, doing the three weekly posts and eventually working with her web developers to update her website further. As much as I enjoyed this opportunity and valued every new skill I was developing, eventually it became too much, as I was taking on more and more paid assistant styling jobs. With a heavy heart I had to resign.

Not even two weeks later I received a call from Laura begging me to come back in a paid position. My replacement had already made so many mistakes that it seemed more reasonable for her to pay me than have to deal with a less reliable unpaid intern.

This is a job I still hold to this day, one I refer to frequently as my freelance job, having held strong through every career swing and health crisis I have encountered since. This business relationship is one of the longest-lasting I have ever had. There is something comforting about having it that makes me feel like even if everything else in the world crashes down this job will still be there for me.

I know Laura feels the same way about me because every time she is in New York we get together and she makes sure to thank me for being the most consistent assistant she has ever had. I pride myself on being a woman people can count on, even if that just means making sure a blog post will be up at 9 a.m. every Tuesday and Friday, in sickness and in health!

Laura could have quickly blown me off, considering I was more of a fangirl than a reasonable fill for the open position. Instead, she saw my drive (desperation) and found a place for me in her business. If I had never sent that email, knowing that the odds were against me, I would not be able to have one of my idols as a boss and mentor.

- How to Sell Yourself -

There are still days when I catch myself scratching my head about why I was hired in the first place, but I'm eternally thankful for standing in RK Bridal every day.

Recently while at work I was in a conversation with a manager about a new girl she was thinking of hiring. This girl had little to no experience, and if we were to hire her it would be for an entry-level position without much responsibility. She wanted to work in bridal, but how could she with no experience? We'll just ignore the fact that I had never sold a wedding dress in my life before this job!

I asked how old she was as we went to look over her application. This applicant and I graduated college the same year (2016). She even had a more relevant degree. But looking down her résumé showed one curious number over and over again: 2017.

I'm sure she worked very hard in school and focused on her education, like her parents most likely pushed her to do. That is great until you start applying for jobs post-graduation and don't have enough experience to fill up half a page on your résumé.

Even the work that pays the bills can put you ahead of the game. No disrespect to those who survive on an allowance. That is a privilege I could only dream of! But that also leaves room for interests, hobbies, and outside activities. Think about the career you are working towards. There is always something you can do to prepare yourself for your future, even before you graduate.

Want to be a writer? Find a local magazine to work for. Want to be a photographer? Find a photographer you admire in your city and ask to be his or her assistant. These could be paid or free jobs depending on how well you sell yourself and the city you live in.

Even if this applicant at the bridal shop may not be getting the job she originally applied for, my manager saw something in her and wanted to take a chance on her. It wouldn't even take long for her to get promoted if she worked hard enough and showed the owners that she's willing to learn.

Having the willingness to learn and grow outside of your job description will always do you good. This is especially true in a smaller company because every person will have to know every part of the business, even how to scrub the toilets.

I can't tell you how often I've seen the owner of RK Bridal roll up his sleeves on a busy Saturday and plunge a toilet that some kid shoved paper towels into.

You may not be qualified, but you are the best person for the position, as long as you make yourself the best person for that position!

Chapter 7: BALANCING WORK AND PLAY IS AN EVERYDAY STRUGGLE

I never really did the whole "crazy college student days" thing. It's possible I'm just a weirdo, but getting a full night's sleep has always been more fun for me than puking in a public trash can and paying for a forty-dollar Uber back home by myself. Okay, that's a bit dramatic, but you get the point. And let's just say I didn't just pull that example out of thin air.

While sometimes it can be worth stretching your wallet a little for a special occasion, it's just as important to plan the night practically. Going out somewhere you know will land you in an expensive Uber at unreasonable hours with a regrettable headache in a bright store the next morning may not be the best idea.

Some nights, like the one in my upcoming procrastination section, are totally worth a little setback, especially when you have the next day off. Good memories are priceless.

In a city as big as Manhattan it can be extremely hard to make friends outside of your workplace. We don't exactly strike up conversations with the group of people waiting for the crosswalk sign to blink on. Sure, sometimes you can meet people at bars, on the subway, or in your favorite deli. It's true that anything can happen, but most of us are cautious about who we talk to. Let's be honest: we tend to spend all of our travel time with headphones on and our minds in the clouds.

We have also all heard horror stories of people who are too friendly in big cities. None of us want to be on the cover of tomorrow's newspaper as a victim of the next unfathomable crime! "Woman Pulled Off Sidewalk and Forced to Watch Homemade Porn for 24 Straight Hours" is not how I want my name to land in the New York Times.

After my painful lessons on boundaries, I started at RK Bridal with bulletproof walls built high around me. It took me well over six months to lower those walls and begin trusting my coworkers enough to grow friendships. The first day I agreed to go out to dinner with them after work felt like a major internal battle finally won. As hard as it can be to learn the delicate balance a colleague relationship requires, it can be worth the trial-and-error phase. Some of my favorite evenings out have been with my RK bridal family.

Work friendships may not turn out to be the deepest you hold, but your coworkers can teach you a lot, give you a hand when you need one, and hopefully make work a place you look forward to going.

As you have already read, befriending my bosses has only led me to heartbreak, rather than success. Although I hate the idea of regret, as I believe you learn from your experiences, especially your mistakes, sometimes I wish those lessons never needed to be learned. Now there is a fine line drawn between coworker and boss. Even though everyone at RK Bridal is family to me, there is a hierarchy within the family that remains respected.

While working freelance I appreciated the friendship of a few other assistant stylists, but those relationships are difficult to maintain because that world is so unpredictable. What is important is always encouraging those who are sticking to their passion. Nothing is more exciting to me than to see people I have worked with in the past work their way up in the industry. Fashion styling may not have been where my path was leading me, but it is still a highly respectable career.

Remember the people of your past because you will never know when you will need them in the future, especially in a freelance career like styling. Keeping up with your professional relationships may seem like a hassle in the midst of a busy life, but it is important to keep connections strong. You never know when you will need someone to inspire you or talk through something you are struggling with. More importantly, these people may need you one day.

Chapter 8:
Procrastinate

Along with stubbornly needing to make my own mistakes, one of my biggest downfalls in life is my natural tendency to procrastinate. Whether this was writing a paper in college or washing the dishes in my tiny NYC kitchen, nothing I don't want to do gets done until it absolutely has to be done. Remember *The 5 Second Rule* book? One day I'll start using that more often.

My procrastination is at its prime when what I have to do involves me going from point A to point B to get it done. Let's say I'm writing a blog on the couch and I have to do dishes, get laundry put away, and deposit a check. First of all, I'd stretch across the couch to the kitchen table (super tiny NYC apartment, remember?) to grab the check, and then I'd deposit it on the Chase Bank app.

After that I'd finish the blog I'm working on, check Facebook, flip over to this book-in-progress, move some words around, and check to see what needs to be done for the website I freelance for. I would quite literally do anything possible to keep myself busy on my computer before standing up to do all of the work I actually need to get done in another room.

A perfect example of this actually befell me while I was writing this section. I was on the couch with my roommate watching some awful

Netflix movie in the background while I started to lay the groundwork for my life of procrastination. Probably 15 minutes into the movie she looks at me and says, "It's early and we both have tomorrow off. Do you want to go get drinks somewhere?" Already in my fuzzy robe and sweatpants with a night of writing ahead of me, my obvious answer was, "Hell yea! What are we wearing?" because there are some things worth getting off the couch for.

It's not my tendency to go out for drinks very often (Why pay 12 dollars for a drink when I can get three bottles of wine at Trader Joes for that much and not have to leave the comfort of my own home?), but I wasn't feeling particularly inspired at the moment, which made grabbing a drink sound that much more exciting.

I'm a firm believer in the idea that everything happens for a reason, so I don't regret taking the night to be out in my favorite part of town, meeting new people and creating new memories.

That night I actually learned that I have one very useful bar skill. As far as I know there's no exact name for my skill, but I am the reigning champion of what I will name Bar Disk Golf.

This excitement is made possible by poking holes in paper coasters and throwing them like frisbees at the line up of liquors behind the bar. If you ring a bottle you get a shot of whatever is in that bottle. I don't know if earning a shot of Sweet Tea liquor is really considered winning, but my competitive side came out strong. This may have had to do with the pregame shots we downed before leaving the house.

I stopped while I was ahead, as in before I got to the point that my face would soon be in the toilet, but the little confidence boost let me leave with my head held high and made my follow-up french fries taste even better than usual.

The moral of this story is, although procrastination may be ill-suited for finals week, it can end up resulting in great content when you're blindly writing your first attempt at a book.

Right? Right.

Chapter 9:
EVERYTHING CAN KILL YOU

As teenagers we all counted down the days until we could fly away from the nest that is our family home. We complained about rules and restrictions and dreamt of the days when there would be no curfew and no one to ask permission for the things we wanted to do.

It's not until we are actually out on our own that we start to wish someone was there every step of the way, telling us what is right and wrong, when to go out and when to stay in, or when to see a doctor and when to just take a nap.

I feel blessed that my family is always a call away. Sometimes I will fall, sometimes I will soar, but I will always need a support system by my side. When I was in elementary school I used to pretend to have a stomach ache so the school would call my mom to pick me up. At 23 I called my mom to pick me up emotionally more often than the school nurse ever called her for me.

Being halfway across the country from my family now can be hard at times since there's nothing like the comfort of home. The distance challenges me to make the best decisions for myself or learn the lessons from the wrong ones.

Some things are inevitable, though, like sicknesses that hospitalize you.

If I learned anything at 23 it is that anything can (almost) kill you. Crossing the street, taking the subway, or even what seems like a simple ear infection. Some of these silent killers will make you bust out laughing, and some will give you a new outlook on life.

What you have to remember is is that whatever you are going through is just a small portion of your life, not your whole life. These are the moments that will teach you to appreciate the little things.

- How to Cross the Street -

While I was nannying the summer before moving to NYC the family I worked for sent me with their oldest daughter, Taylor, to Manhattan for an acting conference she had been accepted into. This was a great opportunity for both of us, as I needed to search for a job and an apartment, and Taylor needed to get dropped off at her classes in the morning and picked up in the evening. Two big dreamers, one Big Apple!

It had been a few years since I had visited my dream city (an attempt to save money in order to actually move there), so on her first day of camp I proudly walked her to Starbucks, all the way to her class, and then made my way over to Times Square to take in the chaos one more time before becoming a grumpy New Yorker who couldn't stand the tourist trap. (Update: it's already happened. Times Square is pure Hell, and I avoid it at all costs).

After taking in the sights for a total of five minutes I started wandering away without any real plan, just thinking about finding the subway and seeing what neighborhoods I could tour.

Mid-thought about which direction I was going and what my next step was, I had stopped at a crosswalk waiting for a construction crew to decide what they were doing. Suddenly my head went from floating in the clouds to full focus on the waitress dressed in all black running late to work.

She had ignored the "DO NOT WALK" signs, as most New Yorkers do, because she was late and didn't have time to worry about whatever construction was happening around her.

It turns out the signs were there because the subway grates that had been there since the infamous Marilyn Monroe dress-in-the-air scene were finally getting replaced.

If you've never been to NYC you should know that these metal grates are what allow ventilation to the hot subway trains below, and they get walked on, peed on (by humans and animals alike), and slept on just as much as any other piece of sidewalk available.

This waitress was so caught up in her texting that she didn't notice the edge of the rusty metal sticking out at her as three large men attempted to carry it across the street. In not-so-slow motion her calf met the corner of the piece of metal at full speed. I was lucky enough to watch the rusty, dirty old piece of metal deeply impale her shin and then promptly get yanked out as she fell backwards onto the sidewalk.

The street went silent as everyone around lost control of their bottom jaws and knees started buckling.

Shrieking at the top of her lungs, this girl demanded an ambulance as the construction workers made sure she understood that this was in no way their fault. Because everyone's first thought is lawyers these days.

Being a trained lifeguard, and probably the only person around with nowhere to go, I called 911 for the first time in my life and sat there waiting for the ambulance.

My basic lifeguard training and Grey's Anatomy addiction reminded me that the first thing to do is apply pressure to the injury. My second piece of training was to never put yourself in direct contact with someone else's blood. Considering it was pushing 90 degrees that day, the only extra pieces of clothing we had between the two of us was her cashmere cardigan, so I wrapped it around her leg and applied as much pressure as she could handle, considering most of the flesh in her leg was inside out at the moment.

As soon as the paramedics arrived I let them take over and looked at my blood-and-cashmere-covered hands. Trying to keep my breakfast down, I asked for something to sanitize my hands with and was handed 100 little alcohol wipes. So much for my day of adventures. It was time to head back to the hotel for the longest and most satisfying shower I've ever taken.

If my memory serves me right, this girl was 23 at the time, and I can also guarantee that she never crosses the street without looking both ways anymore.

This was one of the first moments I realized what real New York life is like. No, I have not yet had to call 911 for anyone else, but every day New Yorkers experience something new and surprising that teaches us something—like not to look at your phone while you cross the street!

- How to Ride the Subway -

I fell through the cracks.

If you've ever been in the New York subway system, you've heard the announcement, "Watch the gap between the subway and the platform."

That announcement is for newbies like me who are so caught up in their own world they make little missteps that lead to lifelong embarrassment.

In the middle of my intern/assistantship with Charlotte I found myself on the east side picking up jewelry one day (nothing good ever happens on the east side except Earl's Beer Cheese). On my way back down to my little storage unit I was caught in rush-hour subway traffic, which has you shoved in so close to everyone around you that you can smell what kind of shampoo they use.

I was by the doors because I seemed to be one of the last to the party. Coffee in one hand and my cell phone with attached headphones in the other, the doors opened at the next stop. As I attempted to politely step off the train to let the passengers behind me off, someone thought I wasn't moving fast enough and decided they'd help me move faster. As I was shoved towards the platform I lost my footing, and my black combat boots found the six inches of empty space between the train exit and the beginning of the platform.

Before I knew it I was on the ground and completely numb. In a whirlwind 30 seconds the girl standing next to me was wiggling my left leg free of its concrete and steel trap while three men behind me were ready to lift me up and plop me back onto the train before I even came to terms with what had just happened.

By the time I had collected myself the train was already on to its next stop. It was all I could do to turn around and thank my guardian angels. The biggest mistake I made, though, was to continue to look around and see that every eye on the car was on me. That was the longest four stops of my life.

The best part of the story? I didn't even spill a drop of my coffee!

- How to Catch a Cab -

New York City may be considered the city that never sleeps, but some seasons are easier than others to navigate a social life. Going out in the winter adds complications that aren't even on your radar in the warmer months.

There's layering: do you wear a big sweater and risk buying your own drinks all night? Do you wear a huge coat over your cute clubbing outfit and then carry it all night? Do you just bite the bullet and pay for coat check?

There's transportation issues: are busses running? Is the train running on delays; will it take you three hours to get to the Lower East Side? Is there an insane surge on Ubers because it's dangerous to drive?

And most simultaneously comical and not funny at all: how dangerous are the icy sidewalks to walk across while tipsy?

It's not often I get out for a full-blown dance night, but when I do I make the most of it. One of those nights happened to be the first snowfall of my first NYC winter, and my friend Danielle and I met a group of her friends out to bar hop. This sounds like fun until the frozen water that's coming at you at high speeds finds its way into your non-waterproofed leather boots.

Despite the numbness, a night out is exactly what I needed during the Charlotte days of high stress and little sleep.

When we settled into a bar the obvious answer to fixing our frozen hands was as many drinks as necessary to warm us up from the inside out. Looking back on this, we may have gone about it the wrong way.

On our walk to the last bar of the night Danielle began to feel lightheaded, so we decided to hail a yellow cab and make our way back to my apartment. I wasn't feeling my best either, so my warm bed sounded like the best idea ever.

While we were in the cab Danielle started to feel sick, but I assured her we would be home soon and could take turns with our heads in the porcelain throne.

As we pulled up to my apartment she was apparently more excited than I thought because as I was paying the cab driver she got out of the car with unmatched enthusiasm while forgetting that the snow had made the ground on my street an ice-skating rink.

The whole thing happened in slow motion, similar to my metro misstep situation, but this time I was an onlooker who couldn't move fast enough to avoid the inevitable.

From the cab I watched her slip from the door of the car, try to catch herself on the snow-covered car parked next to us, slip off of that car-shaped ice sculpture, and fall to the ground, rolling down the hill that is my street. At that point I had skated my way to her but wasn't much help getting her upright and stable.

Walking up the four steps and into the safety of the building was a feat all on its own. I can only imagine how entertained the driver was watching all this go down as he waited for us to get inside safely.

Moral of the story? Get wine drunk at home in the winter to avoid the cold misery that awaits you outside.

Also, sometimes what you need is a good laugh with a good friend.

- How to Stay Alive -

Sometimes a slip-up can't be recovered from so quickly.

You could, one day, go to a walk-in clinic for what you think is an ear infection, hoping for a magical drug that lets you go back to work the next day, and end up in a month-long spiral of hospital visits and bed rest. Or is that just me?

I had found myself becoming a homebody while everyone else around me was in the midst of cuffing season.* I'd go to work, come home, throw on sweatpants, and completely cut myself off from the rest of the world.

*Cuffing season: when the temperature begins to drop and singles everywhere start coupling up to avoid having to freeze alone over the winter. Being single is all fun and games in the warm summer months when there are rooftop parties and beach trips left and right, but as soon as it gets cold we all just want someone to snuggle up on the couch with.

One week I became increasingly dizzy at work and chalked it up to inner ear inflammation, like I had a few times back in college. After a few trips to the walk-in clinic it was only getting worse, and I was getting annoyed because I actually liked selling wedding dresses to women in their happy bridal bubbles and didn't typically enjoy sleeping 20 hours a day.

On my third trip to the walk-in clinic (after an allergic reaction to the meds I was given for my self-diagnosed ear infection) I was straight-up annoyed and looking for answers. Their answer was to send me straight to the ER for a SPINAL TAP! The only people I know who have had those are my now-passed grandfather and cancer patients. Never 23-year-olds with ear infections!

An hour after sitting in the ER waiting room a nurse came up to me and said, "I know you're here for something very scary, but it'll all be okay." Ummm… Excuse me?! I have work tomorrow and am perfectly healthy. Will someone just look in my ear? Instead they drew some blood and let me sit in the waiting room for three more hours with my poor roommate, Dari, whom I dragged with me. And by that I mean I called her from the clinic and said, "They are sending me to the ER. Can you pick me up in a cab, please?" She didn't even see it coming.

Just as soon as I was getting ready to nap on the waiting-room floor I was taken back and told I had about a third of the blood volume of the average human and needed a blood transfusion.

What?

My parents were sitting in Kentucky without power in a bad rain storm trying to conserve their phone batteries to see what was going on with me. Dari had to go to work, and I desperately needed family by my side, so I called my aunt who lives on the Upper West Side, and she dropped everything to be my side. She kept my parents up to date as I answered the same questions from about ten doctors, getting nowhere near closer to knowing what was going on.

Of course this would be the perfect time for the hospital-wide computer system to go down, which meant I had to wait for any sort of medical care. Except rectal exams. The doctors had no problem doing those over and over again. I mean, at least buy me a drink first, guys! Especially considering my first doctor was just about my age, that was the closest thing I'd had to a date in quite a while. Pathetic, right?

That first night I was gifted with many sleepless hours of listening to other patients whining, two IVs in the bend of my arms, and three blood transfusions—not exactly anyone's ideal Friday night. On the bright side, my superhero without a cape whom I call Dad was swooping in to save me.

The real survivor here, though, was my perfectly healthy aunt who "slept" in a plastic hospital chair at the foot of my bed, constantly getting kicked by the husband of the patient just a curtain away. She asked all the right questions and tracked down all the right people when I wasn't alive enough to fight for myself. I can't imagine getting through that night without her. I was pretty much a deer in the headlights—after getting hit.

So my inner vampire was satisfied by the blood transfusions, but what brought it to life in the first place? After a few more days in the hospital I had an endoscopy. This seemed like the answer to everything, when really it became a nightmare of its own.

As I was rolled into the procedure room some nice lady described what they were going to do. She was going to give me medicine to relax me, and then something to forget everything that happened. (Can I get this on tap for every night out I'd rather not remember?) I was hoping for, "You're going to be knocked out cold, and we'll wake you up when this nightmare is over," but I guess the twilight zone she was describing would work too.

As the nurse shot the substance into my IV the world around me slipped away—for a short while at least—until the doctor shoved the ten-foot-long snake back down my throat because he didn't see what he expected to see initially.

I woke up from my twilight zone after the first deepthroat experience. The medicine only lasted the length of a typical endoscopy, but not long enough for them to decide to go back in. It was my own personal Criminal Minds episode as I screamed, sobbed, and grabbed anything I could while the doctor jamming the tube back down my throat had the nerve to say, "Put your arms down and relax. It'll be over soon." Not soon enough, asshole. It seemed as though the drugs they gave me were only for me to *think* I was asleep while being aware enough to follow commands (HELLO, CRIMINAL MINDS).

The look on my doctor's face when I reiterated everything they did during the procedure told me he was clueless to the pain he had put me through.

Guess who demanded general anesthesia for her next two procedures?

What did come out of this experience was a new addition to the medical paperwork. I had a polyp in the part of my intestines called the duodenum. Yes, I had to Google the spelling, and no, I had no idea what that was before numerous conversations with doctors.

This "massive" (according to my charts) collection of unwelcome cells will be called Poly the Polyp from here on out.

During my time in the hospital my dad was staying in New York to be my armor and my shoulder to cry on, but hospital visiting hours were strict, and they kicked him out at 9 p.m. every night. Considering getting actual sleep in the hospital is just about impossible, the ten hours a day my dad wasn't there seemed never-ending. My friends during that time were the phlebotomist who would come by at 6 a.m. every morning to draw blood for tests and my nurses who would stop in every hour or so to check on me. For most of my visit I was NPO, which meant nothing got past my lips besides a few ice chips for about a week. Nothing draws out a day like not even getting to eat.

One bright spot in this week of darkness was learning to truly appreciate the friends who stretched out their hands to me in my time of need. My whole RK Bridal family, who had just barely gotten to know me at the time, were constantly reaching out, and a few of my co-workers even came to visit me. Friends from all different parts of my life were texting me to check on me every day. Family from all over the country were praying for me when I've never needed more prayers in my life.

A friend who really stood out during this time was Matt. I met him when I moved to Kentucky and started teaching swim lessons at the YMCA. He quickly became the big brother I've never had and dealt with me just randomly showing up at his house when I needed a friend throughout my four years in Lexington.

Since moving we always catch up when I'm in Kentucky, but I'm the worst at texting people to keep up with them. As soon as Matt found out I was in the hospital, though, he made it his duty to call me every night when visiting hours were over and I was alone in the hospital room. He is heading into medical school, so he helped me comprehend all the terms being thrown at me from many different medical teams. If I needed to talk through something that scared me he would comfort me, or if I needed a distraction he would tell me stories of the crazy things he had gotten into recently.

Thanks to Matt and all of my other friends who surrounded me from afar I never felt alone in the sterile and stiff hospital bed. Even better, the support didn't end when my hospital stay was over. Co-workers, friends from around the country, and family continually checked on me in the weeks after hospitalization I spent stuck in my tiny Harlem apartment.

My roommates became my nurses and researchers as I slept in the living room for months to take advantage of the strong window AC unit. There's nothing worse than a hot, tiny room when you don't feel well.

At one point about a month into this nonsense at a check-up appointment a nurse asked Dari and me if we were doctors because we knew more medical terms than she did. Sorry, lady, just Google and Grey's Anatomy. (Hi, Dr. Jackson Avery. Will you marry me?)

So after my week in the hospital ending with a quick pancreatitis scare I was sent home with a little more blood and many more questions than I went in with. (I did get discharged with enough time to sit around the Thanksgiving dinner table, though!) The only hope I had to hold onto was a meeting with a specialist doctor in two weeks. That's fine because I could go back to work to distract myself from my lack of answers, right? Nope, I quickly went from good to bad to worse. Any doctor I talked to said there was nothing they could do until this Oz-like speciality doctor fixed me.

Before too long I was back to being in bed 23 and a half hours a day and crying after eating a dinner roll once a day. This was reason enough to go crazy, considering my normal love affair with food.

Every day went by so slowly in anticipation of meeting the great Oz character who seemed at the time to be hiding behind the curtain of

86

nurses and paperwork. He was unreachable yet the only person who could catch me in my spiral.

By the time this appointment arrived my mom swooped in to be my rock, mentally and physically, as I was having trouble standing up and completing thoughts. She carried me into the hospital as we began to unveil the barrage of curtains that we were finally being welcomed into.

After what felt like months of waiting I was finally about to meet the legend who was supposedly god-like in the gastroenterology world.

Leading up to this moment the only control I was able to grasp onto was my ability to pray for a good outcome.

The prayer my mom and I agreed to stick to was that this doctor would suddenly have an opening for an endoscopy during that week before my mom's return flight back to Kentucky. This meeting was important, but all it was supposed to accomplish was for the doctor to gather all of the information about my case.

As we sat in the office of this doctor nervously waiting for him to appear we said one final prayer as the door opened.

Up to that point I hadn't pictured this man as a real person, more as a mythical creature without a face, but from the moment he opened the door all of the curtains dropped. A British man with a pink tie and sweet smile extended his hand for me to shake, and the world started to get just a little bit brighter.

Like many other medical professionals he started our meeting by asking me to tell my story. By this point I had said it so many times it was more like a monologue than a list of health issues.

"It all started when I thought I had inner ear inflammation." But you know that story already.

My pale skin and hunched demeanor told a large part of the story as well.

After a few minutes of conversation Dr. Pink Tie concluded that we needed to get Poly the Polyp out ASAP and turned to his computer to get my next endoscopy scheduled.

After clicking the mouse a few times he stopped, turned to his nurse, and said, "Where is Tuesday on my schedule?"

The day had seemed to disappear off his computer as soon as he opened the calendar.

Mom and I linked hands in a Hail Mary move, as that was the day we had been praying would be the official "evict Poly" day.

Suddenly the day showed back up from being edited by his receptionist.

Someone had just rescheduled their endoscopy, which left Tuesday at 9 a.m. free for me.

I couldn't even look at my mom; I already knew she was crying, and I couldn't have both of us tearing up in front of my guardian angel GI specialist.

Until then I hadn't realized how much hope was an intricate part of my well-being. Before that moment there was nothing inside of me. No blood, no food, and no hope. This made healing next to impossible.

After receiving that news something inside of me changed, and I was able to eat an amazing bowl of tortilla soup, sit up, carry on conversations with my roommates, enjoy a good movie, and do it all with a smile on my face.

This may not sound like a lot, but at the time it was a major step.

On Tuesday I cringed as the needle entered my arm in the same location that was still bruised after receiving three units of blood just weeks earlier. The thing about IVs, though, is that the pain is just a step to healing when you are sick enough to need tubes in your arm.

Dr. Pink Tie came by the prep room as I sat in my hospital gown, holding my hope high on my shoulders. With his sweet British accent and subtle confidence, any nerves I had faded away. It was time to let go and let God.

With my past issue of waking up during an endoscopy I made sure to scare everyone around me into giving me enough drugs that I may not even remember what I had for dinner the night before. My anesthesiologist assured me that there would be no waking up until she was ready for me to wake up. She put some magical cocktail in my arm and a mask on my face, sending me into a dream world.

A few hours later, as soon as I regained consciousness, the first word to come out of my mouth was, "Poly?" and my mom looked at me shaking her head with disappointment.

The world around me shattered. This internal war against my own body wasn't over yet.

Poly the Polyp was more complex than she originally led on and would require more testing. Any hope I had brought into the procedure had been left back in the sterile room. It was back to sleeping 23 and a half hours a day.

My mom had to go back to Kentucky a few days later, and Dari was back in charge (not that there was really anything anyone could do).

This hole in my life I was spiraling down, like a scene from Alice in Wonderland, brought me back to feeling like the rock bottom that was my 23rd birthday.

Finding hope again in both of these situations seemed impossible, but luckily for me I had a solid support system set in place during my best days that stuck with me through my worst days.

My poor family took on another full-time job just checking on me multiple times a day, my sister talked to me more than ever before just to make the time go by quicker, and Dari basically canceled any plans she ever had to sit at home with me.

I will forever be thankful for these four people holding me up when I couldn't stand on my own. It means more to me than they will ever know.

Because of their support I vowed to myself that once I got better I wouldn't put off anything I dreamed of doing.

This book you're reading right now? It's a product of years of dreaming and multiple Google Docs finally put together because it was time to stop saying I wanted to write a book and to put action behind my words.

After six years of blogging I felt like I had more to say than just the short stories and quick tips I was sharing on laurenallen.com.

There is still so much more to learn, but why wait for the future when there are stories to be told right now?
My third endoscopy in a month's time was a solemn one. There was nothing I wanted more than for Poly to be gone and for me to find my new normal, but there was no way I was going to get my hopes up about anything anymore.

Dr. Pink Tie's receptionist told me over the phone a few days prior to the procedure that a polypectomy was scheduled, which sounded promising to me, even though I wasn't totally sure that "polypectomy" was even a real word.

In the prep room the day of the procedure, giving me major déjà vu from my last moments of hope, I sat with Dari, leaning on her to be my backbone when I could no longer fight for myself.

The newest doctor on my case, whom Dr. Pink Tie had brought in as backup, came by my waiting area and informed me that in this procedure they would be taking a few more samples of Poly, and then we would know more in a few weeks.

She didn't know it at the time, but those were fighting words.

Dari started in on the fight, and Dr. Newbie raised her hands in defeat as she walked out to find Dr. Pink Tie.

Once he arrived our tempers eased, and we felt ready for whatever would happen.

I woke up alone in a recovery room since Dari isn't a blood relative, but caught a nurse's attention as soon as I found my voice.

"Polyp?" I asked.

"They took a polyp out during your endoscopy," the nurse said nonchalantly, not knowing the significance behind those words.

I made her repeat this to me multiple times before I believed it.

Poly the Polyp was no longer in my body.

This meant I was no longer sick. I was recovering!

There was still a long way to go, considering there wasn't much muscle or energy left in my body, but it was finally time to start gaining it all back.

Once the anesthesia had worn off enough for me to get up I went to meet with Dr Pink Tie again for him to tell me the good news himself.

Apparently I was some sport of medical mystery because his eyes glimmered with excitement as he proudly told me that Poly was in a jar and he still had no idea what she was or where she had come from. The only thing he could confirm was that the chances of her coming back were almost none.

After that day it was finally time to start slowly introducing my favorite foods back into my life: coffee, wine, hot sauce, and red meat. I was starting to feel like myself again.

My full recovery was finalized back home in Kentucky over Christmas and New Year's, allowing me to hit the ground running as soon as I landed back in NYC in 2018.

- How to Go Numb -

The best part about pain is that the brain holds no memory of it. If it did, why would anyone ever give birth to more than one child?

Sure, childbirth is a beautiful miracle, but I've seen videos before, and there is no way any woman would choose to go through that more than once if her body truly remembered the pain it caused.

I've been thankful for this trait a few times over the years. My tie-in with Dr. Pink Tie held a few of those never-wish-to-remember moments. I've had people say to me since, "You must have been in so much pain! Was it awful? How did it feel?"

Honestly, I have no clue. I remember the details. I remember the fear of those around me. I remember the annoyance of getting poked and prodded. What I don't remember at all is feeling anything.

Sure, there were moments of tears when they had to replace the IV in the crook of my arm. There were sobs when eating lemon ice folded me in half, but as I think back on it all I feel is numb.

If "numb" was to be considered a feeling, anyway. I don't like it all that much more than the physical sting of a needle. It is void of any actual availability of my five senses.

This is your body's way of protecting you from physical and emotional pain.

After my tumble out of LA I fell into months of numbness. At that point it was welcome because any time my senses would start thawing all I could feel was raw, uncut pain. This was the kind of pain that left no physical scars, drew no blood, and could only be seen by those closest to me. At that time I was happy to do anything I could to freeze the pain away again.

Some aches become so consistent and overpowering that they take all memory, not just the pains.

During my sophomore year at the University of Kentucky I woke up one morning with an imaginary knife twisting its way through my intestines.

The scream that came out of my mouth was one I could not even fake in an audition I did for a high school play. My mom and her friend who was visiting Kentucky (I'm sorry to ruin your vacation, Carol) dragged me in a full fetal position to the emergency room, where I was soon told I had a stomach bug and to rest at home.

A week of couch sleeping and minimal movement later and that same scream began to escape my lips. Again I was rushed to the ER, and before I knew it I was appendix-free.

Soon enough I was back to class and living the bare minimum life. Every job I had disappeared, my list of friends diminished, and I had even gotten to the point that my mom would drive me to class every day.

At all of my follow-up appointments with my surgeon, whom I called Dr. Know It All, I would reiterate that something was wrong, but I couldn't put my finger on it. Dr. Know It All reassured me after many tests that he did nothing wrong in the procedure, and, therefore, everything I felt was in my head.

The funny (not so funny) thing was, during that past year both of my parents had had their gallbladders removed, my dad for gallstones and my mom for a non-functioning gallbladder that was extremely hard to diagnose. My symptoms were lining up with theirs, and although I may not have a medical degree, it seemed to me that my gallbladder was the troublemaker here.

Testing for all of this was not as easy as an x-ray or ultrasound. The test that gives you information on the functionality of a gallbladder is one for which you lie on a hard, plastic bed with a long strip of paper underneath you and a large metal box hovering above you.

The person conducting the tests sticks an IV in your arm and begins flooding your body with a number of fluids. First there's the test run just to make sure it's getting all the way through. Then there's the one that makes your insides glow. That must be real natural (#PLANTBASEDPLEASE). After that the fun begins. The final step is pumping you with some sort of liquid whose sole purpose is to pretend it is a massive McDonald's meal, and your gallbladder has to produce enough bile for your body to process that big meal.

The idea is that if you don't react your gallbladder is working just fine. If you feel any discomfort the organ is either not working or struggling to work. My main memory of this test is going from feeling only the prick of an IV in my arm to my whole body cohesively springing off that plastic table in a split moment. I honestly had no idea tears could come out of an eye socket that quickly.

Of all the pain this test caused the one good result I was sure would come out of it was that I would finally have an answer to the question that kept me up at night.

More thrilled than ever, I went into Dr. Know It All's office ready for his admission of defeat.

His response? "The test is not definitive enough to tell me that your gallbladder isn't functioning."

At that point I pulled out the gun I had stored in the back of my yoga pants and shot him between the eyes.

.

.

.

JUST KIDDING! That's just what I considered doing. Instead we got a second opinion from a family friend who also happens to be a general surgeon in Florida. He completely agreed with our diagnosis and suggested evicting my troublemaking gallbladder.

Armed with a second opinion and Mammabear at my side, Dr. Know It All caved in and said, "If you really, really want me to I'll take out your gallbladder."

Thank you so much for your words of encouragement.

I took him up on his kind offer and scheduled the procedure the day before Thanksgiving, thinking I'd have a few days of recovery and wouldn't have to miss any school.

Thrilled to be finally getting the fix I had been waiting SIX MONTHS for, I prepared properly the night before the surgery. How, you may ask? By dying my hair pink.

To those of you who know me now this would come as no shock at all, as my hair has been purple since before I got my job at RK Bridal, but at the time it was a major life change for me—one that made me feel confident, beautiful, and in control.

As I lay in the hospital bed the next morning with my breezy floral hospital gown and my pink locks tied up in a blue surgical cap, Dr. Know It All came up to the side of of the bed, rested his hand on my shoulder, and asked, "Are you sure you want to do this?"

This is when I took the knife I was holding with my other hand below the blanket and stabbed him in the chest.

.

.

.

JUST KIDDING. Maybe I need to stop watching crime shows.

But really, I was dumbstruck as to why this man thought I would think having surgery the day before Thanksgiving would be a fun pastime.

For some reason at that moment I did let him go through with taking out my gallbladder and woke up feeling better than I had in half a year. No, I didn't exactly enjoy the turkey that year, but I'd take a few days of recovery over months of pain and agony surrounding what I loved most in this world: food.

By the time I got back to school it was the week before finals, and I was ready. I had all of my energy back, I could drive again, and nothing was stopping me from finishing the semester strong! After all, I had not missed any classes that semester despite being unable to eat during most of it.

(Side note: I also never wore sweatpants my entire college career, including this sick time. I may not be totally proud of all the grades I earned in college, but I never looked like I didn't care!)

As I sat in the semester review classes I realized something was missing: my memory of the entire semester! It was as if I was sitting in engineering class discussions rather than statistics, American history, and linguistics. Soon I tried to remember what happened to the jobs I had held before getting sick and what I did in my free time. Everything was gone. All of my memory for about four months had vanished. Everything I had was fed to me through social media, my parents, and those semester review classes I was sitting in with a big question mark over my head.

Luckily I had done well enough throughout the semester that my not-so-great finals scores evened out to a passing semester and I didn't have to take any of the classes over again.

In the midst of traumatic times like this it feels like your world is getting smaller and whatever you are going through is taking over for good. Seeing past the pain can be harder than seeing through the eye of a hurricane. It is devastating, but it only lasts for a short period of time.

As much as I hated Dr. Know It All and everything I went through with him, that experience helped prepare me for what was to come, Poly the Polyp. I would have probably never have stepped foot into a hospital on my own without having been in the past for my appendix and gallbladder.

Chapter 10: Single in the City

This is the part of the book where I would like to give you dating advice. In reality I am the last person who should ever be giving dating advice. At 23 most of us are balancing on a tightrope, attempting to walk from college to career with gusts of wind pushing us between enjoying the single life along the way and hearing, "When do I get a son-in-law?" from our mothers. (Shout out to my mom for being both of those gusts, depending on the day). Despite my best attempts at dating, so far I have yet to find myself in a consistent relationship long enough to share any good tips and tricks.

I almost didn't write about dating because it just makes my eyes roll with a mixture of laughter and dred at how little I really know about relationships after countless attempts at playing the game and trying to follow the ever-changing rules. Although I've failed at the game every time I have thrown myself into it, the attempts have left me with plenty of stories to tell.

- How to Stay Single -

Before moving to New York I avoided dating to the best of my ability. At times I would get tired of seeing everyone around me madly in love and start putting feelers out to see what my options were. The issue that kept blocking any attempt at a love life was that my biggest fear in life was getting stuck in a small town.

Growing up I had heard stories about how falling in love meant your sense of practicality dissipates and the only thing that matters in the world is being with that person. These stories were more like fairy tales, but in reality I was afraid of falling in love and falling away from the career I had spent so many years working towards. The last thing I wanted was some man with slick southern charm to sweep me off my feet and keep me locked away in my hometown because there is nothing for him in the city that never sleeps.

I had decided I wasn't meant to fall in love until I moved and was too far into my career to change my path for a relationship. A downside to this mindset of waiting to fall in love in New York City is that I then expected to get my first set of keys to my Harlem apartment, make my way through a few weeks of styling, and then be presented with the most perfect lineup of men ready for a committed and happy relationship.

My first dating experience after moving seemed like that perfect romance movie, or at least the opening scene of one. I was just days past my first-ever interning day when I officially caved and bought a pair of Adidas sneakers, still a little uncomfortable with the idea of wearing sneakers outside of the gym. I was on the subway in those stark white kicks with black stripes freshly out of the box when I heard someone say, "I like your shoes." My first reaction was to assume the statement was not directed towards me, as I was wearing sneakers with jeans and there was nothing cool about that. This was the last day I felt unsure about how attractive sneakers were; before I got to my stop that complimentary voice had gotten my number and asked me to get drinks later that week.

When the day came I was in a panic, starting to regret ever agreeing to margaritas in the first place. Sam seemed perfectly nice over text, but I had no idea what to expect, and I wasn't sure I would even be able to recognize him in a new situation. I was more nervous about this date than I had been about steaming priceless Oscar de la Renta gowns the day before.

As I walked into the upscale Mexican restaurant on the Upper East Side my eyes drifted towards a man sitting by the window wearing a crisp button down, dress pants, and a tan leather belt that matched his dress shoes in the way you would see in a luxury car commercial. I waited for a spark of recognition in his eyes before making my way over to the plush chairs to begin a night of official introductions and small talk.

The night went smoothly and ended with him kissing me goodnight at the entrance to the subway after I insisted he did not need to order me an Uber because he had already bought my drinks and I was a strong-willed New Yorker (of almost two weeks). As I was lying in bed that night I was pretty sure this was exactly the relationship I'd been waiting all my life for and that God had answered my prayers for a quick and easy dating life.

It wasn't long before I realized the spark of the first day would die down quickly as he filled our texts with excuses of being a broke, busy, and tired medical student. Sam was in his last semester, just weeks away from leaving the city for an undetermined residency somewhere in the United States. Unfortunately if I saw him at all after that first date he was either in basketball shorts or his scrubs and white coat. (I have to say, the Grey's Anatomy lover inside of me melted a little every time I saw that white coat.) That "love affair" ended quicker than it started, considering the romance movie I was picturing got paused after that first date and no other official dates followed. In reality neither of us were in a place to start new relationships.

I could partially blame myself for the dead-end romance since I was just starting in the intern styling world and I had never been more physically exhausted in my life. At that time holding a conversation also meant holding my head up with my hand. By then I was really just dipping my toes into the industry and was not ankle-deep like I had planned. Once Sam officially moved out of the city I hit pause on any attempt at dating because I had realized the styling world didn't allow for any sort of scheduled activity.

- How to Set Standards -

Even with a more set schedule these days, having traded the freelance world for the bridal shop, I still dread first dates. Before dates are officially scheduled they always seem so exciting with the endless possibilities of outcomes and outfit choices, but once the day comes not all of these possibilities are so thrilling.

There seems to be a war right now between feminism and chivalry. Girls are stronger than ever these days and do not need anyone to define us, but most of us appreciate acts of chivalry in ways that men show they are respectful gentleman through their actions. Due to this guys are now claiming to be afraid to hold the door for the girl who caught their eyes at the deli out of fear they'd get their knuckles slapped for assuming a girl couldn't hold the door for herself. No, I'm not making this up! I have been told by multiple men that they are afraid of participating in chivalrous acts because they have been scolded for them in the past.

Some men use feminism as an excuse to be lazy and cheap when it comes to dating. It's rare to find someone who will walk you home when it's late to ensure you get back safe or even walk you to the nearest train station if you are far from home. From my perspective the ones who do are the ones worth keeping around a little bit longer. It shows they actually care about your safety. I always appreciate someone going above and beyond in their actions to show me they care. It's easy to talk the talk, but following through or doing something without looking for anything in return will always be the sexiest thing a man can do.

From my experience the best way to meet some of the least chivalrous men around is through the use of dating apps. We've all tried them. Some people have met their significant others on them, but most are just left with horror stories of Tinder dates past.

Technology is truly amazing, but it sure is easy to use it to get lazy. There are so many bars, coffee shops, and subway trains in New York City that it can be overwhelming to think about always being on the lookout for your next big crush while going about your day.

As much as I love sitting at my local coffee shop on my days off to write and stare at all the young businessmen who pass through, I'm not really the type to start conversations, and I'm also the first one to put on headphones and bury my nose into my MacBook to get work done rather than socialize.

My preference is to curl up on my couch later that night with a bowl of popcorn and scroll through the latest dating app I saw an ad for on Facebook earlier that day. It seems so easy to be able to hand-pick men from a selection of thousands who are seemingly single and looking to date. There's no wasted time making eye contact with the man across the room to see if he'll come over and ask for your number or flash a gold band wrapped around his left ring finger that you couldn't see because his beer was in the way.

The problem that seems to get in the way of finding true love through an app is that many of the men who are desperate enough to put themselves on said app aren't exactly worth writing home about. The majority of them are either looking for sex within the hour or aren't willing to leave their PlayStation controllers long enough to mingle in the real world. There are also never-ending choices on these apps, so it can seem absurd to stop at just one when there is always someone new just one swipe away.

The idea of the Bigger Better Deal is blanketed over the dating world, especially in New York City. With over 8.5 million people living on this island and easy access to the surrounding areas, convincing someone you are the only one for them is not the easiest task.

Why would a man agree to be with just one woman when there are six trying to dig their claws into him thanks to the odds that there aren't even enough men for every woman in the city?

The BBD of dating is that if there's one good one who's to say there isn't a great one just around the corner who could do what the good one does but even better? Funny enough, having requirements cuts the options significantly until you think the perfect person only exists in novels.

The amount of single men who are just as unqualified for a good job as they are to be in a serious relationship is frightening to single women everywhere.

My dating threshold is a little different than some. I want the man I end up with to treat me just as good, if not better, than my dad treats me. If you don't hit that requirement nothing else matters, and I don't need to keep you around. #sorrynotsorry

My dad calls me the "World Famous Lauren Allen" every time I walk into a room. If a man doesn't make me feel that special he's not the one for me. They say you marry someone like your father. I am looking forward to that. He is the most generous and smart person I know. He never lets me settle for "just okay," and when I want to he finds a handful of ways for me to go above and beyond and doesn't let me stop until I have gone the extra mile. Yes, I did get extremely lucky in the dad department.

Even if you don't want to hold a candle to your dad, look for someone in your life who makes you feel special, whether it's an uncle, brother, or someone who might as well be your brother. Use them as the threshold for your dating standards, and don't let them fall.

I want to end up with someone who always pushes me to do more, love more, and dream more. Having fun, getting lost in time, and forgetting responsibilities is fun every once in a while, but that's not what I want to base a relationship on.

Millennials are known for having short attention spans. This gives us a bad reputation from older generations who did not grow up with 100 different forms of media coming at them from every direction. At times this can be a negative quality because it's easy to walk away from something before finishing it, but that also means that if we do it right we can accomplish multiple tasks at once. Having a short attention span can really mean being able to juggle smoothly. I personally can't juggle anything real to save my life, but I can successfully juggle writing a blog post on my computer, researching how to market to millennials, and shopping on Amazon Prime, all while watching Friends in the background.

This trait can become troublesome in the dating world, especially in a big city like Manhattan. With countless dating apps, bars that are open until 4 a.m., and supermodels casually walking the streets, finding someone and keeping them can be harder than finding a rent-controlled apartment. (Side note: I have neither.)

As consumers we are constantly looking for the next best thing, and that doesn't stop at sneaker trends. Don't let dating become the next trendiest aspect of your life. Know what you want and put your time into the ones who fit the bill. This also means not letting the fun, trendy guys distract you from someone who could stick around long-term.

I struggle with taking this advice myself, at times getting swept away with promises and big ideas even though I know better.

We will all have different experiences with the BBD, whether it's feeling our eyes start to wander or trying to hold the attention of the person we are attempting a relationship with. I think your biggest take-away from this is just knowing that it is spreading like wildfire through the dating community.

- How to Swipe -

I've had a few different types of dating-app first-date interactions. By "a few" I really do mean a small amount. Although I have downloaded and deleted multiple apps since moving, it is rare for any of the matches to evolve into an in-person meeting.

What I learned about myself the hard way at 23 was that I become increasingly desperate for attention when I do not feel well. I don't mean the common cold; it's more like when my body is working against itself to kill me. I found myself looking for someone to tell me I'm pretty, smart, and worthwhile when I couldn't tell myself those things. Yes, I am talking about the beginning of the Poly the Polyp era.

During my slow decline before I knew I was sick and just felt useless dating apps and sweatpants filled more of my nights than skinny jeans and good friends. The more I swiped left on all of the "hell no" options the more my standards would get just a little bit lower wanting to find one person to swipe right on for the sake of a match. Eventually I matched with Chris, and my instincts told me it was either going to be a hit or a total disaster, considering he shared a name with my dad.

We chatted back and forth for a few days before he asked if I would like to meet him for dinner that Saturday night. I said, "yes," looking forward to having a reason to get dressed up after work (post-nap, of course). He chose an Italian restaurant in the middle of Brooklyn and told me to meet him there at 8 p.m. It had been longer than I'd care to admit since someone had asked me out on a dinner date, and I was nervous about sitting directly across from a stranger and having a conversation while also trying to look attractive eating a bowl of spaghetti. I didn't know it yet, but the fact that I was slowly internally bleeding wasn't helping my self-confidence much either.

Over an hour subway ride from my apartment later I arrived at this restaurant. It turned out he worked in the city but lived in Brooklyn, and that's how we matched, even when I tried my hardest to avoid seeing people who live outside of Manhattan. We started with a drink at the bar while we waited for a table and then made our way over to the back corner of the dark restaurant. I was starving and feeling a bit light-headed after the first drink, but could not get myself to dive into the delicious food. I was too nervous I'd somehow do something wrong.

It turns out that as much as I was carefully watching my actions throughout the night, so was he. The post-dinner course turned into my date psychoanalyzing me and telling me all about how I act on a date. He broke down everything I had said, explaining exactly why I had said it and what it meant. I felt like I was on What Not to Wear for dating where they would secretly film me and then tell me everything I did wrong afterwards. In the middle of this lecture he asked for the check and then immediately put his card in the envelope before it even hit the table. Not having been in this situation very often, I wasn't really sure what to do, but I went along with it and thanked him for the delicious dinner.

A few days later I met him for coffee on my day off when he finished with work. He told me how proud he was to finally have a good Monday-to-Friday job and that it was a lot of energy for him to meet people after work during the week. I tried to argue that although it was really exciting for him to have his dream schedule I had met him after work when I also had to work the next morning, so if he wanted to date me one of us would always be coming from work. He didn't seem too bothered that I would be exhausted every weekend when he wanted to go out because seeing me during the week was just too big of a hassle for him.

He paid for his coffee and dramatically stepped out of the way, using both hands to usher me to pay for my own like a flight attendant explaining the locations of the emergency exits on a plane. Yes, I can absolutely pay for my own coffee, but I couldn't figure out why this guy was making such a big deal about such a small gesture.

As we waited for our lattes he said arrogantly, "I never, ever pay for a girl's coffee. It's ridiculous of them to ever think I would in this modern age." I thought it was a little ridiculous that he would have such a strong opinion on the subject and that he would generalize me with all the other girls he had ever dated when this was barely our second date. That first sip of coffee seemed a little extra bitter that evening.

Towards the end of this coffee date he looked like he had something to say that he'd been holding in for the last hour. I told him to spill what was on his mind, and he started his next sentence with, "So I was talking to some of the women at my office about our date the other night."

We all know that nothing good can come out of that statement.

He told me he was concerned about why I didn't do the "wallet dance" when the check came because all of the girls at his office swore they always at least pretend, if not insist, to pay at least their half of the bill on a date.

It took a minute for me to fully comprehend that this grown man had approached a group of women in cubicles to ask them if they would have offered to pay for dinner on a first date. Not even that, but then he felt the need to meet me for coffee to tell me that my first-date etiquette was wrong according to women who probably would have agreed with anything he said just to get him to shut up.

He also wanted to share with me that we would never work out as a "real couple" because he only dates girls he could bring home to his parents or to Christmas parties, and girls with lilac hair didn't fit that description. I'd also like to note that his parents were both dead and he was Jewish. He was using non-existent examples as excuses for why he didn't want to be with me. That date was more of a race to see who could end things first before they even really started.

It wasn't obvious to me at the time, but my confidence was so low (because of the internal bleeding I didn't know I had) that I let a man treat me terribly.

Just a few weeks after this painfully awkward date I was in the emergency room getting a few late-night blood transfusions when my phone lit up with a "Hey, what up?" text from him. If I hadn't had an IV in the crook of each arm I might have responded, filling him in on my life crisis just to make him feel bad, but instead I cleared the notification and never spoke to him again.

I never fully believed the power of a near-death experience until suddenly none of the little things in life mattered anymore and all I cared about was ensuring my family and close friends that yes, I will be all right.

From now on I think I'll let my dad remain the only Chris in my life.

- How to Desperately Seek Tall, Dark, and Handsome -

That dating attempt was very much over, but once I got back to my regularly scheduled life it didn't take me long to return to swiping out of late-night boredom. A few dead-end conversations left me frustrated with the lack of male ambition in Manhattan's online dating platforms.

Eventually that perfect mix of tall, dark, and handsome popped up onto my phone screen, and I said a quick prayer as I swiped right on his profile. We matched immediately and got to chatting. The messages turned into plans, and about a week later we were set to meet for drinks after work.

He picked a spot that was outside of my typical comfort zone in the city, but I was happy to try someplace new. After work that day I re-powdered my nose and started my 30-minute commute to the Lower East Side. It took me longer than expected to get there, but that was okay because he was also running late.

The bar was basically empty when I walked in, so I picked a seat with a view of the front door to make sure he would see me when he walked in. For the first 20 minutes I told the bartender I was waiting for my date to show up before I ordered.

After 20 minutes I decided to order a cocktail because if I was being stood up I might as well be sipping something delicious. As I took my first sip a group of chatty men walked up to the bar to order a round of drinks. One stopped and asked me why I was drinking all alone on this beautiful day. I filled him in on the story and we toasted to dumb boys.

A full 45 minutes after our planned meet-up time I took one final swig of my pink martini and flagged the bartender down for my check. Before he could get to me the front door swung open and in walked Mr. Tall, Dark, and Handsome. The gay man I had spoken to earlier and I each looked over at him and then at each other with our jaws on the floor. Finally, a man who looked even better in person than in pictures!

He quickly apologized for being late as if it were a five-minute differential, and we began with the regular first-date conversations. The next hour went smoothly, and I was fully interested in going on another date with him, but something inside of me was telling me I should have left before he arrived and made him reschedule. I left him to go to church, unwilling to change those plans for a guy I had just met, and we parted at the train station with tentative plans to see each other the next week.

Whether he knew it consciously or not, my guess is that he lost respect for me being the girl who is willing to wait the better part of an hour for a first date. I never heard from him again and have yet to go on another date with someone I met online.

That date was a learning moment for me about never being too available. This is something I need reminders of at times when I get bored, but I did use the word "desperate" in the title of this section for a reason.

- How to Please Your Mom -

I am not the only one getting a little tired of my consistent singleness, though. My mom lovingly wanted to help me find a son-in-law for her once I had gotten back on my feet after my 23rd birthday fallout, so she suggested (urged) for me to try a Christian dating site. I was a young, churchgoing, Christian girl looking for the same in a man, so it made the most sense out of all the dating sites.

My dad cringes a little every time my mom asks about where my future husband is, happy to let me be single for the rest of my life. The thing is, the more he cringes the more fun my mom and I have talking about it just to drive him crazy. No, she is not pushing me to just find someone and settle down, but something about turning 23 brings the beginnings of the "marriage and kids" questions.

I reluctantly filled out the form online one particularly boring afternoon and started to scroll. Soon I realized that filtering my searches to men in their mid-20s to 30s living in Manhattan also narrowed down my options significantly. It also didn't take long to figure out that even if I was interested in one of them I needed a paid membership in order to have a conversation.

After a phone call with my mom trying to convince her that if she wanted a son-in-law so badly she should pay for this membership she told me with a smirk in her voice that I wouldn't put my all into the website unless I was putting my own money into the project. It was worth a shot at least.

With a loud grunt and a small side of whining I said, "Fine," and started typing in my credit card information. Was I really at this point? Well, I had already tried and failed at joining church groups. No matter how hard I tried I just could not get myself to talk to people around me at church, so this was what my life had come to.

Being very sure that handing over a wedding dress worth of commission money would land me in a dress of my own with just a few clicks on a Christian dating site, I started to scroll through my newfound possibilities.

It turns out that paying for access to this not-so-selective group really only allows you to view the messages that were previously hidden from desperate 50-year-old men who use the word "Christian" lightly. In the two weeks I actively used the site I received more inappropriate messages from men than I ever have on any "hook up" app before. The disappointment only grew when I realized that almost every person my age who would catch my eye lived in Connecticut. Before the next monthly charge came around I screenshotted all of the messages I'd received and demanded my money back, and for those people to be flagged in hopes they could be stopped before coming on to the next girl who logs in.

Customer service jumped right on my problems and gave me a refund without question. I'm sure this site has helped many people find love, but it sure wasn't right for me.

- How to Feel Too Tall -

So online dating just is not for me. How about I meet people the more natural way, at a bar with a little bit of liquid courage running through my veins?

My next best guess was that if I spent time in the part of town where I would eventually like to live maybe I would meet someone who already lives there. Lively sports bars on the Upper West Side became my go-to for four-dollar gin and tonics and casual conversations. This is also where I had my realization that there must be something in the New York City water because there are days when I can walk in and look over the heads of every person in the bar.

Being five-foot-eight, I have always been the tallest of my friends, but my dad is six-foot-five, so that is what I assumed most men were also. We all know what happens when you "ass-u-(&)me" though. A vast majority of the men I come across in this city are five-foot-seven or below, leaving them with an unfortunate view of my double chin.

Going out with my roommate is always entertaining, as she is a little five-foot-nothing Puerto Rican with big curly locks and I stand almost a foot taller with long purple hair running down to my bra line.

As we sit atop bar stools our stature isn't as obviously different, but I am sure people question how two girls who are so different could be such good friends. Some let their curiosity get the best of them and bring their beers to our little corner of the bar to say, "Hi." Usually they wait for one of us to get up to go to the bathroom before approaching the one who's sitting alone.

One typical night a group of three men had been watching us from across the room and decided to strike on Dari while I was in the bathroom. As I snuck back into the group they were deeply focused on the conversation and didn't realize I was the lost friend until I made myself back at home on my stool.

The five of us got to talking, laughing, and sipping on fresh drinks. Before long the men asked if we would like to follow them to a different bar. Dari and I looked at each other, then to a quick sweep of the rest of the prospects at the bar, then back to each other and said, "Sure, I guess so," as this bar was dead.

We jumped off the stools, collected our bags, and headed for the door. This is when the moment of realization hit. Even the tallest man in the group, who would obviously be the one I would talk to the most according to the girl gang rules of my best friend and me, was only tall enough to make eye contact with my boldly colored lips. The shortest would only be Dari's height if she slumped her shoulders. Even if any of us could deal with a little awkward height difference, this was just too much.

Just like a game of tag, all three men tried to get her arm as quickly as possible in fear of getting stuck with the giant (me). One politely tried to have a conversation with me on the walk but soon got tired of straining his neck upwards and ran over to whisper in Dari's ear that he had tried, but I am just too tall.

Is it only southern men who get both the gentleman gene and the tall gene?

Needless to say, we accepted one more free drink as payment for the strain of doubling our chins to look down at them and never saw the group again.

Every week is a new wave of "I don't care anymore. Single life is great!" and "Maybe tonight is the night I'll meet the man of my dreams!" while swiping on my favorite shade of berry lipstick.

What I do know for certain is that the perfect man for me is out there somewhere. I have no idea when I will meet him, where I will meet him, or even what he will look like, but at the right time our paths will cross. Some days I have more patience than others; it really all depends on how many newly placed engagement rings I see on Facebook or how many brides at work ask me if I'm married yet.

Until then dating is all trial and error just waiting for something to stick. I wish I could give you some solid advice on the best ways to date at 23, but if everything I have done has led to me sipping a glass of Two Buck Chuck in an oversized t-shirt on a Saturday night by myself, then all I can tell you is that the only Trader Joe's in New York City that sells wine is in Union Square.

Chapter 11: HOLD TRUE TO YOUR FAITH

Faith is defined as "complete trust or confidence in someone or something."

Having faith to me means trusting yourself to know what is right and wrong and holding what is right as gospel. That is unwavering faith. If you go through life questioning your choices, actions, and values it is easy for other people to come in and influence you into doing things your gut knows are wrong.

Ever since I can remember I knew eventually I would move to New York City. Over the years my short-term plans have changed, and flaming curveballs got thrown at my beautifully organized life calendar. The only aspect that never changed was my unwavering goal to land in Manhattan.

All I could do was hold true to my faith in knowing that one day I would end up in the city of my dreams, as long as the work was put in during every step of the journey.

Sometimes wrong decisions are made, sometimes things out of our control can go wrong, but no matter what the bigger plan is always secure. You might not even have a clue about what your bigger picture is, but that's okay because God does. If you let him, he will lead you along the way. It's all about doing the best you can with what you have and letting the rest fall in place.

Trust me, this is so far from easy some days! It can be easy to fall out of faith when things seem tough and you are drowning in everything the world seems to be throwing at you. What you won't know until it's over is that it is never as bad as it seems. There is resolution and happiness on the other side.

- How to Keep the Faith -

Since moving to Manhattan my faith has been tested constantly and in ways I never could have imagined. At times this made me question my beliefs, which pushed me to look further and dig deeper into what all of this religious stuff meant to me. In the end all of my digging just brought me to a stronger relationship with God.

This doesn't mean there aren't moments of weakness. I get frustrated and question why so many bad things could happen to me when I work so hard to get down the path I think God has laid out for me.

Turning 23 flipped my life upside down. It seemed that one thing after another would come to strike me down and every time I got back up another punch would come from an angle I never expected. No matter how many times I would want to tap out or raise a white flag it was never an option because this is life, and life doesn't stop just because you called for a timeout.

Many new long- and short-term goals had also been set for myself that year as I weeded through the negative parts of my life and left only what made me happiest.

Setting goals has always been a kind of comical move for me. It seems that every time I have some amazing plan in mind for myself I am working hard towards God laughs at it. As I can see the end in sight He throws a wrench into my plan. At first this is always frustrating and disappointing, but before too long something better than I could have ever planned happens.

With the amount of times my college plans changed it's a real miracle I graduated on time. Three different schools in two different states, all with different requirements. Add in the fact that I'm a terrible test taker and never liked school in the first place, and the piece of paper now hanging on my wall is quite surprising.

At least once a semester I would beg my parents to finally let me drop out to start my career just a little bit early. Thankfully they always said, "No" and told me to get back to studying. They kept reminding me that it wasn't necessarily about what I was learning in school; it was about proving that I could stick to something for four years without giving up. Of course I learned many things and met many amazing people along the way, but on the worst days what I needed was to prove to myself and others that I can stick to something through the end.

All I could do was trust that they were right and pray that the real world was more enjoyable than the college world. In reality college is a hell of a lot easier than the real world most days, but it is a step along the way for many of us.

At 23 it was a little more difficult to see the bright plans that shined ahead for my future. It felt like going from having courtside seats to being forced into the nosebleed section of my own life. I would still always hold onto my self-laid plans until something else came along, but as soon as I would see myself getting closer to them some sort of obstacle got in the way.

After my Poly the Polyp crash I really thought there could be nothing else that could come up to put me out of commission. That was all the sick days I needed to take for the next few years.

Not long after telling everyone around me that I was better than ever and thriving I woke up one morning and my biggest fear was back. I just knew that Poly had returned and Hell had fallen on top of me, crushing my chest and breaking my heart.

The day after attending a huge bridal show with the RK Bridal family I had to call Mrs. RK from the ER because something was wrong and I couldn't go to work the next day.

All of my tests came back normal that night, so they sent me home despite my gut telling me otherwise. A few days later I met with my favorite doctor, Dr. Pink Tie. He worked his magic and got me into my fourth endoscopy just two days later.

I wish I could tell you I went into this procedure with full faith that everything was going to be all right. In reality I went in with little hope of a good outcome in an attempt to guard my heart from more disappointment.

Turns out that everything had healed since he took out Poly and my insides were better than ever. This was great news, except I still didn't feel right, and no one could help me.

Am I losing my mind? Is Poly PTSD a thing?

That feeling passed eventually, and I was back to work confused but ready to sell wedding dresses. I was working, writing, socializing. It was everything I moved here to do.

By this point in the story you should know that there is always more to come.

My life was starting to feel like that race I wasn't going to finish without cuts and bruises along the way.

This is also the reason I didn't run track in high school (besides the part where the only reason I see to run is if someone is chasing me with a knife). I used to watch these long-legged people sail down the track and jump over poles that were put in their way to trip them up. Why would you do that for fun when the chances are high that you would eat pavement before finishing the race?

- How to Find Peace through the Pain -

During my second year in New York I came closer to death than ever before.

When they say, "What doesn't kill you only makes you stronger," they are not kidding. After battling thoughts of suicide, my own body fighting against me, and my own city trying to eat me alive, my will to succeed is stronger than ever right now (most days).

My stories may be truly one-of-a-kind, but we all have struggled to climb mountains that have made us stronger and given us new perspective once we got to the top.

Obviously that's just a figure of speech because there's no way you'd see me on the top of a mountain unless a helicopter dropped me off there.

Scariest of all the struggles are the threats coming directly from inside your body that you can't prevent or diminish on your own.

My own body has been out to get me more often than any outside source! Every time I land back on a cold paper-covered chair in a doctor's office I ask myself what I could possibly be doing wrong in life to end up back here. The hardest answer to accept is the one where you realize there is nothing you could have done differently to change the situation.

There are also people who come into your life and get under your skin so much that you don't see the purpose of living anymore. Sometimes they don't even know the impact they are making, but their words cut like knives deep into your skin, and the scars left behind change how you see yourself forever.

All that can be done in these situations is to use the pain to push yourself to be better. Realize that sometimes life gives you a second chance because you have more left to do than you ever knew.

It's the pain that thickens our skin for what is yet to come.

As much as I would like to try, it is impossible to be ready for anything that comes my way. Sometimes something happens that you could never prepare yourself for, like your whole jaw locking up after spending an hour working with a bride. The frustration of never feeling healthy despite doctors telling me I was fine hit me as hard as the jaw pain, and I left work early that day with deep sobs flowing out of me.

The next day I went to a chiropractor in an attempt to find a more holistic healing approach. We began a long-term treatment. After a few weeks I had left work in tears more often than I had left pleased with my hard work for the day. I was also seeing my chiropractor more often than I was seeing my friends.

Since I was young my mom has had jaw pain, and I knew it ran in the family because when I was in the hospital with Poly I was diagnosed with TMJ (Temporomandibular Joint Dysfunction; yes, I did have to Google that). Every once in a while it would sneak up on me, but it was nothing a glass of wine at the end of the day couldn't heal. I assumed this was the problem, but deep down I knew it was something more.

Something. Was. Wrong. As much as the Chiropractor, icing, and wine drinking was helping, it just wasn't enough.

By now my gums were swollen over my back teeth, and every time I closed my mouth it irritated the gums more. It was time to find a dentist in NYC.

It took three days and a lot of outside help, but I found a dentist's office near my apartment that was walk-in and took my insurance. At the moment I was dog sitting for my Upper West Side family, so the next morning I walked Barkley early to ensure I could get to the dentist as soon as they opened.

Three hours of sitting in the waiting room later the secretaries convinced my insurance to cover the appointment, and I went back for x-rays. A few slobbery pictures later, the dentist came in, shook my hand, and told me it was nice to meet me, but that it was time for me to leave. My wisdom teeth were impacted, and I was at risk for infection if I didn't get them taken out as soon as possible. He picked up the phone in the room and called his oral surgeon friends to ask if they could take me in that day. They agreed, and he sent me on my way.

I went home and broke the news to Dari, who was trying to enjoy her day off. This girl never gets a break from my illnesses either! She grabbed her tote bag, computer, and coat and followed me over to the office.

Ever since I can remember I've had a fear of getting teeth pulled. Not the dentist in general! I've actually always enjoyed getting my teeth cleaned. But the idea of someone pulling teeth out of my mouth and leaving me with massive craters in my gums makes my skin crawl, so as bad as it was to have to do this all without any warning, I was thankful for not having any time to panic about the procedure.

I was especially thankful to not have time to freak out after the dentist told me I had two extra wisdom teeth and would need a total of SIX teeth pulled that day. Was that possible? Would I ever be able to eat steak again?

After another three hours in that waiting room, waiting for my insurance company to cooperate, and a dog walk for Dari and Barkley, I was nearing panic, but just before it hit in full I was sedated and no longer in control. When I woke up Dari was waiting for me, and I was ready for the fun times you see in YouTube videos. It was about time I went viral for something, right? Instead I was hit with immense pain and eight shots of Novocaine in the dentist's best attempt to get me out of his office in one piece.

I apologize to anyone in the waiting room who had to hear my screams before their own wisdom teeth removals.

The numbness had worn off by the time I was snuggled up with Barkley, and all I could do was pray for the pain meds to kick in faster.

Another day of calling Mrs. RK to tell her that another emergency had popped up and I'd need a few more days off work. If I was so over these sick days she must have been too!

Two days later my chipmunk cheeks and I were back at the bridal store looking more pathetic than ever, but eager to work. The brides that day must have felt sympathetic; every woman I worked with bought a dress, and one mom even gave me the most generous tip I've ever received!

This was the best selling day I had ever had, and all I knew for sure was that I had God to thank as he picked me up from my latest fall. There were still many wounds to be healed, but it could only go up from there.

Over the next few days I still had moments of crippling pain and extreme frustration over the lack of foods I could eat, but this was the answer to a lot of the pains of the previous weeks, which meant the end was in sight.

While getting ready for work four days post-op, listening to Ed Sheeran, tears began flowing seemingly out of nowhere. As I tried to stop myself I realized this was build-up from the last week or more and it was just time to let it all out. I put down my makeup brush and joined Barkley on the couch for a good cry session. Through the tears I couldn't get my thoughts in order, so I grabbed my laptop and opened a blank document.

Over the next ten minutes I wrote a letter to God asking him why it seemed like every time I began making progress on the path He had laid out for me something would throw me off course. Was this all a part of the plan? Was it the devil seeing me doing His work and getting scared?

Being a firm believer in the idea of everything happening for a reason, I knew to trust the path, but I didn't know how to explain it.

Why would I continue to fight and believe when it seemed like my own body was fighting against the idea of me succeeding? It was becoming increasingly disheartening to even dream when there never seemed to be a break in my health issues.

Maybe it was just time to quit all of the excess and just do the minimum to get through life with as low of a profile as possible.

If this book and my ministry in faith was really something I was to continue I needed some answers and fast.

There had to be a reason for all of this, or there was no point.

After finishing that letter I re-washed my face and jumped in an Uber to work, where I would be spending the day learning a whole new part of the company that was far outside my job description.

This was obviously my idea of the perfect activity just days after removing six teeth and not having consumed real food since then. The upside was that it allowed me to sit down at a computer and just type for a few hours without having to smile and make small talk with customers while I barely had any function in my face.

On the way back to Barkley that evening I was listening to Brian Houston's (Hillsong Church's lead pastor) new book, *There Is More* on Audible when suddenly every question I had asked in my letter was being answered in just one small chapter of his book.

The biggest idea that hit home with me was that "disappointment produces perseverance, perseverance produces character, character produces hope, and God-given hope does not disappoint."

All of these disappointments that keep tripping me up in life are really just lessons to make me stronger for the future. God is also pushing them now while I am still on my parent's insurance, which is saving me thousands of dollars in doctor bills.

It may not always be easy, but if you hold true to your faith God will bless you in sometimes weird but always useful ways. It's easy to question His motivation in the hard times; you just have to remember that He can see a big picture that you will never be given access to until it becomes your past.

Bad things happen to all of us. It's just what you do with the lesson that will impact your future immensely.

- How to Overcome Weakness -

The first time I saw God clearly in my work at the bridal shop was with a "difficult" bride.

She wasn't difficult because she was rich and picky like you may have seen on TV before. She was just more complicated than most. At all of her past bridal appointments she had been told she was too fat for wedding dresses.

This beautiful woman had no confidence in her ability to find a wedding gown simply because she hadn't been able to try on any of the samples. This was mind-blowing to me! It's not reasonable to have every size available in every sample, but there should always be enough options for every woman to be able to see herself inside a wedding dress.

Bridal shops typically have one of every dress in what they consider a common size. This is usually around a size 12, which in street clothes is about an eight. Luckily this works for about 70 percent of our clientele, as anyone ranging from sizes zero to 16 can typically get a good idea of how the dress will look in their size.

For those girls who fall in bigger sizes there is a different section. Not any better or worse, just a larger sample size. We call this section our "diva" department.

After working with Jane for about 20 minutes, putting her in the small samples she had picked out, I could feel her pain. The sadness radiated out of her, and it broke my heart.

Everyone deserves to feel like the most beautiful girl in the world on her wedding day, and this poor girl didn't think she would ever get that feeling.

As I ran out to the sales floor to pick out a few more dresses I said a silent prayer: "Dear God, even if Jane doesn't buy a dress from me, please give her the confidence she needs to radiate beauty on her wedding day and every day around it. She is a kind, loving, and stunning person. She deserves to see herself as her family and friends do."

The next few dresses I brought in fit her like a glove, and suddenly her shoulders drew back and her chin lifted up. As the final dress zipped tears fell down her rosy cheeks. We stepped outside to show her family, and before we knew it all of us were crying. She said, "Yes!" to her dress that day.

Jane taught me that it's not the dress. It's how you feel in the dress.

We are all made in God's likeness, which can be easy to forget while constantly bombarded with images of what the media defines as "perfect."

There are plenty of moments I look at myself in the mirror as I'm clipping a bride and think, "Ew! Look at that fat roll on my stomach," or "I should have used concealer on that blemish this morning."

Luckily my fellow bridal consultants are some of the most encouraging women I've ever met and boost my confidence even on the days when it seems nowhere to be found.

It's not possible to go a day in RK Bridal without someone commenting, "Have you lost weight?" or "I love that lipstick color," or even something as silly as "Why do you look so pretty today?" Working in an environment so uplifting makes such a huge impact on the rest of my life. It also makes me want to do the same for my clients every day.

We have to show our brides their true beauty through our wedding gowns, and if that doesn't work I call in backup. Prayer has helped me sell more dresses than I could have ever imagined, but it's not the numbers that mean anything to me. I am happiest at the end of the day when I know every bride I worked with has found a wedding dress that makes her feel sexy, confident, and eye-catching.

There are days when the perfect dress just doesn't exist in our store. Not every day will be filled with happy tears and giants hugs. It's the Janes in the world who make my job so fulfilling.

At 23 it can be almost impossible to not look around and compare yourself to others' success, looks, or relationships. What you won't always see are all of the people behind you looking up to you. One of my favorite sayings when I find myself feeling behind in life is that the only person you should try to be better than is the person you were yesterday.

- How to Find Light in the Dark -

By now I have told you about my latest heartbreaks and struggles, but let me tell you about the first man to break my heart.

It was the end of the spring semester in my junior year at the University of Kentucky.

I was working with my mom doing makeup for a beautiful bride one Saturday morning, and as we were packing up we got a phone call that would change the next month and rest of our lives forever.

My grandpa, Pa, as we lovingly called him, had been in and out of the hospital for lung problems. This most recent admission seemed just like the many others, quick and simple. He was 85 and a frequent flier of Baptist Health since moving into our Kentucky home, but we were all very sure he was way too stubborn to die any time soon.

Until the phone call came in telling us that he had terminal skin cancer. Not exactly something we ever expected to hear.

Once my mom hung up the phone we threw everything in the back of her car, and I drove us to Pa's bedside.

I have a tendency to hold in my emotions until they forcefully find their way out, and that day was no different. We were in the next town over for this wedding, so the drive back was about an hour and a half. The whole ride to the hospital my eyes were dry, and my mind was on the road. I couldn't even think about glancing over at my mom, knowing her face was damp with fresh tears as she swallowed the news of her dad nearing his end. This was the same man we had to trick to even get him to the ER in the first place, the same stubborn Irishman who just a year earlier had driven 18 hours in a U-Haul from Naples, Florida to Lexington, Kentucky, not letting his perfectly capable son take the wheel.

No emotions passed through me along that long stretch of highway. That is, until I pulled into the hospital parking garage, shifted the car into park, and sobbed harder than I had ever sobbed before. This was the first time I had ever come close to losing someone I was so attached to.

Once I pulled myself together we went into the hospital and sat with Pa as we talked to the doctors about what the foreseeable future looked like. Because God is really the only one who can make those kinds of decisions it was really a waiting game from there on out.

We sat with him for the day and then came back at every possible chance over the next few days while his doctors tried to get him into hospice, but he was denied multiple times because he never stopped eating. This comes as no surprise if you know our family!

That is, until the world flipped upside down that Monday.

Something was off about that day, and I couldn't quite place the feelings. I went to my classes and found myself crying through all of them, which is far from my regular MO. My professors kindly pulled me into their offices and told me to go home, but I am not the person to miss class, and I had an important meeting that afternoon.

After my last class I locked myself in the bathroom and cleaned up before my meeting.

This was the day I would find out whether or not I would get the paid internship at our school fashion magazine, KRNL Fashion, that I had been dreaming about. It was everything I had ever wanted, the title of key stylist for a fashion magazine. It wasn't Marie Claire, but it was as close as a college student in Kentucky could get.

As soon as I walked into the office I re-lost all the marbles I had just spent the last 15 minutes collecting (no surprise there). What did surprise me, though, was that on this painful day I also gained my dream college job.

I couldn't believe it. Could something this good really come in a time of so much pain?

Later I would learn that God works in mysterious ways like that.

As soon as I got the news I ran straight to my car and flew over to the hospital. Luckily I was only a few stoplights away or driving may not have been the best choice that day.

Since moving to Kentucky Pa had become the first person I went to with exciting news; his pride seeped through his skin. He always supported my crazy dreams and goals.

The best part about Pa, a part that none of us totally appreciated until it was gone, was how he had a story for everything. No matter what I did, as millennial and new-aged as it may be, he had a story about growing up on the farm he'd use as a lesson or a laugh to match my story. Many of the stories were repeated, as most of his life was spent either on a farm or building swimming pools, but that's okay because they are now embedded in my brain forever.

With my exciting news in hand I walked into Pa's hospital room for what I didn't know at the time would be his last day on Earth.

Pa greeted me with his biggest smile, even behind his oxygen nasal cannula and all the wires and tubes covering his body. I sat down next to him on the bed, held his hand, and told him about my new job, what it was, and how it would impact the rest of my career.

He cheered for me and spoke the last words he ever said to anyone before his illness overtook him and he became someone else for his last few hours on Earth.

He said to me, "I am so proud of you."

Who knew six words could make such an impact?

Moments later in the blink of an eye my Pa was gone and someone else took over what was left of his body. His nurse had moved him to the rocking chair, and I was sitting on his bed writing a final paper for one of my journalism classes. That year I had become particularly comfortable studying in his hospital room.

Suddenly he said to me sternly, "Pick that up!" and pointed to the empty space next to me on the bed.

I asked him what he meant. He just repeated his statement, so I picked up the laptop I had closed when he spoke up and said, "Do you mean this?"

He replied, "Yes! Now pick up each side."

So I opened the laptop again, confused as ever but following directions.

"Now tape the bottom shut, put it on the ground, and start the next one."

It took me a few minutes of this imaginary building to realize that we were packing moving boxes because he was getting ready to leave us.

As soon as we had packed up all of the boxes he wanted me to I grabbed my phone and stumbled into the hallway, finding it hard to breathe or wrap my head around what had just happened. I called my mom, who had been there just an hour before I got there, and told her to drop everything because she needed to be at the hospital. Now.

When I hung up the phone my knees went weak, and I fell to the floor in sobs. Dr. Compassionate happened to be walking down the hallway while I was in the middle of my episode and came over to talk to me. He said there was no way to know how long this version of my Pa would last, but his gut (that he technically wasn't allowed to share with patients) told him today was his last day.

After I pulled myself together for the umpteenth time that day I walked back into the room just soon enough to hear about the amazing Chinese architecture that was surrounding us in that room, including the brass pipes and high ceilings.

By the time my mom got to the room the nurse had helped him back to bed and given him pain meds that let him rest for a few hours.

Still not knowing what to expect, except what our guts had been telling us, we sat around Pa and prayed because there was nothing else to do at that point.

We told Pa that more family was on the way and to just try to hold on for the official goodbyes.

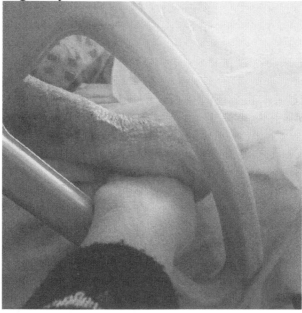

I will never forget the feeling of him squeezing my hand in his sleep as I laid my head next to him late into the night. We typically didn't stay with him overnight, but I wanted to so badly, so my mom agreed to stay with me.

That is, until she sprung up in the darkness and said, "We need to go home."

I didn't know why, but at that moment we packed up our stuff, kissed him goodbye, and dragged our sleepy bodies back home.

Not ten minutes after arriving home and plopping onto the couch with a glass of milk to ease our worried minds Mom's phone rang.

It was the hospital calling to say that Pa had died while a nurse sat with him soon after we left.

The stubborn old man didn't want any of us around when he died!

We ran downstairs to Grandma, who was sitting at her kitchen table, phone still in hand, taking in the news she had just received. Her husband of over 50 years was gone.

Just days later our home was filled with family and lifelong friends.

The funeral was beautiful and painful at the same time. We followed the traditional Catholic funeral with the one component we knew Pa would have wanted: an Irish wake.

It was Kentucky Derby day, so we bet on horses, drank gin and tonics (his favorite drink, and now my go-to), and ate more food than we thought was even possible.

This day brought us together as a big family more than any other event ever had. Any family disagreements dissolved, and distance shrunk. We were family, and that's all that mattered.

Since then I have seen and visited with family members all over the country whom I would have never even known if Pa hadn't brought us all together in that time of deep sadness.

Pa taught me to make the best of every bad situation because no matter how painful it seems there's always joy on the other side and stories to tell around the kitchen table later on.

Chapter 12: Finding Your Miracle

In my first few weeks of working at RK Bridal I had this gut feeling I just couldn't shake.

It was the furthest I had been from the darkness of my 23rd birthday and the first time since moving that I was very sure I was exactly where I was supposed to be.

So if I was where I needed to be, what was this feeling I couldn't shake? The awareness that something big was around the corner ate away at me like acid.

Every Sunday after work I would go to church with my ears open and phone off, ready for God to tell me exactly what that next step in my life was going to be.

Was I soon going to become Instagram famous? Was I going to be given the opportunity to travel around the world? Was it finally my turn to get a reality TV show? I don't even really watch reality TV, but it seems like something people get excited about.

I think what He was telling me was to hold on to that faith for just a little bit longer because before I even realized it I was hospitalized, and it turned out the gnawing feeling inside of me was more like Poly the

Polyp being ripped open in my intestines rather than my impending fame. But you know that whole story by now.

This was a hard time in my life to hold true to my faith. How could anyone praise God while withering away in the ER with two IVs shoved into the bend of each arm? Not knowing what was wrong, but being told that if I had waited another day to walk into the ER I could have died— these are the times when it's easy to feel like God isn't around anymore.

They say God never gives us more than we can handle, right? Maybe this is something I just. Can't. Handle. What if this is more than fits on my plate? But what if this is exactly what I needed to grow my plate and extend it to be able to take on more than I could have before getting pushed to my breaking point?

There were moments I was sure my breaking point was hit and I didn't know how to put myself back together again. It surely was impossible. Those are the times God shows himself in the people surrounding you. For me this has been my aunt who sat with me overnight in the ER, Dari for bringing me to countless doctors appointments, and many other friends and family who listened to my breakdowns over the phone when they couldn't be in New York with me.

There was one especially empty moment in my hospitalization when I was alone and the events of the past week hit me like a subway train. I had just found happiness in my life, and all that left me with was a near-death experience. Crying quietly to myself into the sterile hospital pillow I prayed that someone would walk in before my throat closed up and breathing was no longer an option. Suddenly I opened my eyes, and a resident who was working on my case was standing at the foot of my bed asking, "Do you need a hug?" which was exactly what I needed at the moment. I'm not even sure if that's allowed or not, but he saved me from myself in a moment when the devil was working his way into my head.

If there are any times I can feel my faith slipping God appears in someone around me, and all it takes is the realization that although life isn't always fair it is beautiful, and the best is just around the corner.

Once I finally got back to my normal routine after getting sick I went back to Hillsong Church, and the title of the sermon that week was "On the Border of a Miracle."

When I first think of the word "miracle" my mind goes to the bible stories where Jesus healed the blind and parted the Red Sea. If those are miracles how can any of us be on the border of one when we're just average humans trying to get through life with as few scratches as possible?

What I have to remember is that miracles are all around us in the simplicity of everyday life. They are pushing through to accomplish something you never thought possible, giving a meal to a homeless person, or even something as small as offering a compliment to someone you may not have known was on the edge of suicide.

This brought me back to the feeling I was having before my whirlwind sickness. What was my impending miracle I was on the other side of? I could see the sharp corner but never what was around it. Poly couldn't have been the only thing brewing inside of me!

The funny thing was that all along I was gathering content for this book.

It didn't have a name, chapters, or a purpose, but the Google Doc was growing steadily. Suddenly it hit me that *How to Be 23* was the glue meant for putting together all of the pieces of my life.

I had been blogging for five years with nothing much to show for it besides 800 plus posts and countless outfit pictures. It's something I have been and always will be proud of, but more for personal reasons than to say I reached a broad audience.

How to Be 23 is exactly how I wanted to reach people my age and say everything that's been placed on my heart for so long now. Maybe I'm crazy and only my family will read it (Hi, Mom and Dad!), but at least I can say I followed through with something I felt totally and completely passionate about. For years I've been saying that when I'm older I will write a book, but why wait when life if so full and confusing just in the first year post-graduation?

My greatest hope is that all of you reading this book find something within it that sparks your passion and pushes you to pursue it without feeling like you are too young, undereducated, or not qualified. No one is more qualified to tell your story than you are, and I know for a fact that we all have our own stories to tell, just like my Pa.

Made in the USA
Lexington, KY
02 June 2019